LITTLE PLAYS OF ST. FRANCIS

VOLUME III

BY LAURENCE HOUSMAN

SAINT FRANCIS POVERELLO. (Messages of
the Saints.)

SELECTED POEMS.

THE LOVE CONCEALED. (Poems.)

THE WHEEL: a Dramatic Trilogy.

THE DEATH OF ORPHEUS: a Play.

THE CHINESE LANTERN: a Play.

THE DEATH OF SOCRATES: a Play.

YE FEARFUL SAINTS. (Nine one-act Plays.)

With H. Granville-Barker

PRUNELLA, or Love in a Dutch Garden:
a Play.

Sidgwick & Jackson Ltd., London

LITTLE PLAYS OF SAINT FRANCIS

by
Laurence Housman

VOLUME III

London
Sidgwick & Jackson Ltd.

LITTLE PLAYS OF ST. FRANCIS

Complete Edition in Three Volumes

First published 1935
Vol. III, 2nd Impression 1944
4th Impression 1947
5th Impression 1952
6th Impression 1955

Applications regarding the amateur acting rights of these plays should be made to the Secretary, League of British Dramatists, 11 Gower Street, London, W.C. 1.

Printed in Great Britain
by T. and A. CONSTABLE LTD., Hopetoun Street,
Printers to the University of Edinburgh

CONTENTS

VOL. III

LITTLE PLAYS OF ST. FRANCIS

LITTLE PLAYS OF ST. FRANCIS

1922. FIRST SERIES :—

The Revellers	The Builders	The Chapter
Fellow-Prisoners	Brother Wolf	Brother Juniper
Brief Life	Sister Clare	Brother Elias
Blind Eyes	The Lepers	The Seraphic Vision
The Bride Feast	Sister Gold	Brother Sin
Our Lady of Poverty	Brother Sun	Sister Death

1923. FOLLOWERS OF ST. FRANCIS :—

Cure of Souls	The Fool's Errand
Lovers Meeting	The Last Disciple

1926. THE COMMENTS OF JUNIPER :—

The Peace-Makers	Makers of Miracle
The Mess of Pottage	The Order of Release
Brother Ass	The Last Comment

1931. SECOND SERIES (in addition to the plays in the two foregoing volumes) :—

The House of Bondage	Gate of Life	Holy Disobedience
Juniper's First Sermon	Juniper's Miracle	The Odour of Sanctity
Gate of Death	The Temptation of Juniper	

1934. FOUR PLAYS OF ST. CLARE :—

Good Beating	Weaker Vessels
Kind Comfort	Holy Terror

1935.

Naked Truth	Blind Heart	Bond of Fellowship

Now added :—

Sister Agnes	Fine Feathers

(All the above plays are published separately, in paper covers, price one shilling net each.)

AUTHOR'S CORRECTION

In the plays *Brother Sin* and *Sister Death*, to conform with Franciscan usage, for the word 'Prior,' wherever it occurs, read 'Minister.'

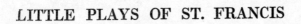

LITTLE PLAYS OF ST. FRANCIS

THE SERAPHIC VISION

On a plateau of rock, high and precipitous, a small cell, roughly built of stones and timber, stands amid a group of pines and cypress-trees. Above the door is a narrow window slit; on the gable a wooden cross. A narrow foot-bridge of primitive construction connects the plateau and the foreground, which is formed of rough stones inter-spersed with juniper bushes. Below the foot-bridge is a precipice, from which emerge the tops of pines. When the scene opens it is dusk; the warmth of daylight has gone, and behind the cell the moon has not yet risen. BROTHER LEO stands alone by the foot-bridge, gazing toward the cell, the door of which is shut. BROTHER BERNARD enters hastily. BROTHER LEO raises a warning hand, without turning his eyes from the point on which they are fixed.

BERNARD. Ha! Brother Leo?

LEO.   Hush! Speak low; speak low!

BERNARD. What canst thou hear?

LEO.   Nothing! . . . Nothing!

BERNARD.   Since when?

LEO. Alas, 'tis three days, Brother.

BERNARD.   Thou hast been here?

LEO. Or Brother Angelo. We watch by turn: And all this while silence as of the grave!

BERNARD. I will watch too.

LEO. My message found thee. When?

BERNARD. At yester-noon.

LEO.   Thou hast been quick.

BERNARD.   Ah, Brother,
Do we not love him ?

LEO.   He is more to me
Than life.   God pardon me !   When I need comfort,
I speak *his* name.

BERNARD. Three days, thou sayest ? and all that
   time no sound ?
Truly, he is within there, think you, still ?

LEO. He is there, Brother.

BERNARD.   And yet liveth ?

LEO.   Yea,
He liveth ! . . . Oh, fair Brother, pray for me !
I may not leave him.   Yet am I afraid !

BERNARD. Why ?   For what cause ?

LEO.   Lest with these sinful eyes
I may behold a mystery too great !

BERNARD. God gave thee thine eyes, Brother.

LEO.   Yea, and my heart
Also ;   yet I do fear !

BERNARD.   Hark, who comes here ?

LEO. 'Tis   Brother   Angelo ;   he   bringeth   bread
Daily. . . . Ah, me !

Enter ANGELO : *he goes up to the door of the cell,*
   stands and makes a gesture of distress.   He ex-
   changes the loaf he carries for the one he finds there.

ANGELO [*returning*]. Look, he hath eaten nothing !
What ?   Brother Bernard ?

BERNARD. Aye. . . . This for three days !

LEO. He hath had no food for seven.

BERNARD. I will go in.

ANGELO. We may not.

LEO. So we watch helpless !   Shall it never end ?

BERNARD. What surety have ye, Brothers, that
    he lives still ?

LEO. I know ! I know !

BERNARD. How knowest thou ?

LEO.   I have seen.
When all is dark, there within wakes a light !
And as a flame before the Sacrament
So through the night it burns, and fades at dawn.

ANGELO. I also have seen it, Brother.

BERNARD.   Oh, what is here ?
'Tis marvel that thou tellest.

LEO.   Why, so I think !

BERNARD. What else ? For surely in thy face
    I read
More than thy speech reveals.

LEO.   Well, thou shalt hear.
On the fourth day, as I watched here alone,—
Nigh spent, for Brother Angelo had not come,—
About this hour, I looked, and lo, the door
Wide, and he standing by it. Then I heard
His voice, ' Who art thou, Lord ? ' and then again,
' Who art thou ? ' and therewith such tender words
Of adoration as I may not utter.
Then said he, ' What am I ? O poor vile worm
That dieth, unworthy servant of my Lord ! '
And as I looked I saw come down from Heaven
A torch of fire most beautiful and bright ;
Over his head it rested ; and from the flame
Came forth a voice ; but of the words it spake
Naught could I understand.

BERNARD.   And then ?

LEO.   What else
I saw not : for by the brightness of that flame

Mine eyes were blinded, and fear shook my heart.
When I awoke, 'twas Brother Angelo
Stood by me ; and the place was dumb.

ANGELO.   Here lying
I found him, Brother ; and when he opened eyes
He did not know me ; only afterwards
He told me this.

BERNARD.   What mystery hast thou seen ?

LEO. I have seen holiness ; therefore am afraid.

BERNARD. Ah ! be not troubled, Brother ! Let
us pray,
God's light be in our eyes, and in our hearts.
Had we but hearts like this, what light were ours !

[*They kneel. Behind the cell the moon rises
among the trees. The window of the cell
lightens.*

ANGELO. Oh, see ! see !

LEO. Oh, is not that light—wonderful ?

BERNARD. Now the door opens.

ANGELO. Hush !

[FRANCIS *appears in the doorway. A pause.
He moves forward, rapt, with face raised and
arms stretched wide.*

FRANCIS. O Thou Lover of my soul, why dost
thou call me
Whither I cannot follow thee ? . . .   [*A pause.*
                                      Yea, I come !
I sleep ; but my heart waketh. 'Tis the voice
Of my Beloved, saying, ' Open to me ! '
O my sweet Lover !

BERNARD.   Nay, Brothers, let us go !
This is too holy a mystery for our ears.
Come, come, away !

ANGELO [*softly*]. Father, God give thee peace !

LEO [*softly, with a gesture of valediction*]. Ah,
little Father, hold me in thy heart,
And pray for me !

BERNARD.   Quick ! ere he speak, be hence !

[*They go out softly one by one.* FRANCIS *stands,
rapt, then speaks with pauses. His voice is
low and tender.*

FRANCIS. I opened to my Beloved, but He was
gone. . . .
I sought Him, He could not be found. . . . I called. . . .
He gave no answer. . . . Be not Thou far off !
O Lord, my strength, haste Thee to succour me !

[*Slowly the radiance of the moon passes into
cloud; the form of* FRANCIS *becomes dim,
only his face is discernible. As he speaks, a
deep vibration of music begins, barely audible.
Everything that surrounds him gradually fades
away; his body seems to stand no longer on
earth but cloud.*

I know, I know that my Redeemer liveth,
And at the last shall stand upon the earth.
Though with corruption worms destroy this body,
Yet in my very flesh shall I see God.
Him shall these eyes behold, and not another :
Yea, though He slay me, I will trust in Him.

[*A pause ; very faintly in the distance thunder
is heard.*

All things were made by Him. And without Him
Nothing was made that was made. In Him was
Life ;
And Life—the Light of men. And the Light shines
In darkness ; and the darkness knoweth it not.

[*Soft sheet lightning begins to play, but the
  thunder is still scarcely heard.*

That was the true Light, lighting every man
That cometh into the world.   All flesh shall see it

[*A prolonged flash of lightning.   After it the
  light grows brighter ; and a fuller music is
  heard, accompanied by thunder.*

O light of heaven, that with a million eyes
Dost visit space, a timeless traveller,
And wing-wide coverest the brief lives of men,
Say, hast thou seen the Passion of my Lord ?
O freshening air, that through a million mouths
Hast given to mortals breath,—air, which He
    breathed
While yet on earth, and which my lips taste now,—
Say, didst thou taste the Passion of my Lord ?
O dust of the ground, trodden by feet of men.
O broken bread of clay, from which was made
Man in God's image, meek substance formed for all,
How hast thou shared the Passion of my Lord ?
O ye great hills, wherefor did ye mount up
High-headed into heaven to gaze on space,
If in that hour ye sought not Calvary ?
Say, saw ye then the Passion of my Lord ?
O ye green things of Earth, ye covering leaves,
And tender herb, and shaken grass, and flower,
Ye drops of dew, ye mists, and sundering clouds,
Ye falling rains, and streams, ye downward torrents,
Ye firmamental tides which ebb and flow,
What part have ye in the Passion of my Lord ?

[*The lightning becomes more incessant ; the air
  around him is charged with golden points of
  fire.*

8

THE SERAPHIC VISION

O winds, His ministers, O wheeling fires,
And charioteers of space which, at His will,
Do burn continually on unseen wing,
Legions on legions, angels that attend,—
Where hold ye hid the Passion of my Lord?
Why doth not Earth sweat blood, if to her dust
From those dear Veins one drop did ever fall?
Why runs not ocean red, since water washed
His Wounds for burial? Why are not those thorns
Ruddier than rubies which once pierced His Brow?
Oh, why is Earth still Earth, since He, from Heaven,
Her Maker cometh giving life to all?

> [*His utterance becomes swift. In the air about
> him a mysterious commotion is seen, and the
> lights no longer burn steadfastly: they gloom
> and brighten again, as though unseen forms
> were passing before them.*

Ye, that with wing on wing
Your faces covering,
Do shroud the hidden thing
From the blindness of man's sight,
Undo, unloose again,
Holy and without stain,
His glory: let Christ reign,
And all be Light!
By birth, blessing, and bliss,
Creation did mean this,—
Form came for Love to kiss,
Making the whole world His!
To Chaos, a waste of shame,
Through night without end or aim,
Into the darkness came
His Word as a shaft of flame.

In silence of night and sleep,
Through the void under, above,
Lo, the Spirit of Love
Moved on the face of the deep ;
He spake, and the Light did leap !
He saw, and it was done ;
He found for its fires a way ;
He parted the moon and sun,
And out of the night brought day.
He made new Heaven, new Earth,
And lo, where the Light did shine
Came living things to birth,
With music, and mouths of mirth,
And eyes to behold His worth,
And hearts to know Him divine.
Was not Creation this :—
By birth, blessing, and bliss,
Clasping His Feet, we kiss ?
We are hers ; she is His ; . . .
He is mine !

> [*As* FRANCIS *ceases, a golden rain is seen falling
> about him ; slowly the air begins to brighten
> with the coming of dawn. Music is heard
> and voices singing. He stands rapt and
> expectant.*

VOICES. Holy, holy, holy, Lord God of Hosts,
Heaven and earth are full of Thy glory ; Glory be
to Thee, O Lord most high !

FRANCIS. O Maker Christ, O Love made Flesh,
make me !
Fashion me in Thine image ere I die !
That I may know Thy Passion, let me be
Partaker of Thy pains ! Weak, weak I cry ;

10

Oh, come Thou unto me !
I faint, for Thee I thirst.   Now, lest I waste,
Let me be filled with thee !   Sweet Saviour, haste,
Lift Thou me up. . . .
Give me Thy cup . . .
To taste !
> [*A marvellous brightness falls upon the face of
> FRANCIS ; the air becomes blue and radiant.
> He stands in a golden shower, gazing intently
> before him. Slowly he lifts and extends his
> arms in the form of the Cross. His voice be-
> comes faint with joy and ravishment.*

O Day-star from on high,
Out of yon Eastern sky,
How swiftly Thou dost fly ! . . .
And lo, with hands stretched wide,
Like my Lord, ere He died,
In form most glorified,
Thou comest ! . . .
From what height ?
O blessed, holy sight !
O Light of Light !
> [*He stands entranced in ecstasy. The dawn lies
> golden about him. From the world below
> comes a loud singing of birds. The mist fades
> and begins to disappear ; behind him is seen
> faintly the cell with its door open. Earth
> appears again. Slowly he lets down his hands,
> which bear the marks of the Passion.*

CURTAIN

11

BROTHER SIN

A large cell containing table, chair, stool, and writing materials. Before the crucifix, to one side of which hangs a curtain, BROTHER LEO *stands in an attitude of deep dejection.* BROTHER JUNIPER, *entering from the outer door, halts abruptly and stands watching him.* LEO *beats his breast; his lips move fast in prayer, but no sound comes from them. Suddenly he stops, and with a despairing gesture draws the curtain across the crucifix.*

LEO. So—so shall it be with me for ever !

[*Moving away, he sits down at the table, his head bowed, his hands clenched before him.* JUNIPER, *approaching softly, stands looking at him.*

JUNIPER. Brother Leo. . . . [*He waits : slowly* LEO *raises his head.*] Shall I tell thee what thou art ?

LEO. Aye ! If thou canst.

JUNIPER. Thou art a fool. [LEO *is about to speak.*] Here ! Do not answer ! for thy wits are better than mine : and if thou talk I shall be beaten. On holy obedience I charge thee, speak not till I have done ! Look at me : this is Brother Juniper—a fool, a numskull. Thou canst tell from my face that I have no brain. Had God not loved me, I had better never been born. When I weep, men laugh that I do it so ill : and when I laugh they are like to weep, I do it with so ugly a face.

But God loves me ; and whether I laugh or weep, He knows what I mean. . . . But 'tis not of Brother Juniper I speak now. Thou moping fool ! [*Then, with softened voice*] Thou dear son of Father Francis, whom he loves best of us all. . . . [LEO *bows his head and the tears rush from his eyes.*] Aye, weep, weep ! Thou dost well to weep ; and canst do it better than I . . . but not with more love, Brother . . . in thy heart.

> [LEO *raises himself. With one arm he covers his*
> *eyes ; the other he extends as if groping for*
> *aid.* JUNIPER *continues to expostulate.*

What hast thou been doing to thyself, these three weeks ? Aye ; ever since thou and he came back from the mountain. Wast thou so mum to him up there ? No wonder he fell ill of thy company !

> [LEO *rises, and turns away.*

Well, this is all I would say to thee—then let thy tongue be loosed. If thou do not open thy heart, Brother Leo, thy heart will die.

LEO. It is dead already ; and by this time it stinketh.

JUNIPER. The Lord give me another nose, then : for I smell it not !

LEO. O Brother Juniper, I thank God for thy small wits and thy great heart ! To thee will I speak. [*He crosses himself.*] In nomine Dei !

JUNIPER [*crossing himself*]. Name o' Jesus !

LEO. I look on Him whom I have pierced, but do not love. My love is earthly ; so am I lost for ever !

JUNIPER. Name o' Jesus : say it again ! You do not love our Father Francis ?

LEO. Would God I did not love him so well ! For when we worship the creature, then is the

14

Creator not in us ! . . . Brother Juniper, I have told thee my grief.

JUNIPER [*shaking his head*]. I cannot mend it, Brother : but Father Francis can. Open to him !

LEO. To him ? I dare not !

JUNIPER. Then thou dost not love him.

LEO. O Juniper, I have seen a mystery done in him whereof I may not speak : therefore my heart is full of fear. For now he is made perfect, and full of light. But what he sees I cannot see. So, looking on him, I know that I am blind.

JUNIPER [*at a loss*]. Eh ! I am a fool again, Brother, and have naught to say. Yet, could I lend thee some of my foolishness, 'twere easier for God to mend thy wits. [*He turns to depart, then faces about again.*] Brother Leo, give me thy blessing on what I am about to do.

LEO. What is that, Brother ?

JUNIPER. I go to feed swine.

LEO. God be with thee, Brother, and give thee peace.

JUNIPER. And my swine also ! Peace for them.

[*He waits till the other speaks.*

LEO. . . . Yea ; and thy swine also ! [JUNIPER *goes out.*] But for me no peace. Darkness is upon my soul. Nowhere can I find Him. Ah, Father Francis, Father Francis, bring back to me the love of Christ !

[*The door of the inner cell opens.* FRANCIS *appears ; he totters and leans upon the door-post for support. His hands and feet are bandaged ; when he walks it is with pain.*

FRANCIS. Brother Leo, come and give me thy hand—for my feet fail me.

LEO [*going eagerly to his aid*]. Let me carry thee, Father ! Where wouldst thou be ?

FRANCIS. Over there, Brother. [*He starts to walk.*] Three steps, . . . and three more . . . and then . . . only three more.

LEO [*tenderly*]. Sit down, Father.

FRANCIS [*seating himself*]. You, too, Brother Leo ; I would have you write for me. Where is the scrip you made yesterday ?

[*LEO goes and fetches it from a recess.*
LEO. Here, Father.

FRANCIS. Read ; what comes last ?

LEO [*still standing, reads from the parchment*]. 'Therefore, let no man say " I love God," if he do not the will of God ; or if he give not his body unto pain of death, that so God's will be done in him, if by infirmity he cannot of himself. So in his weakness shall the power of love be made known. . . .

[*As LEO reads, for grief of spirit his voice breaks.*
FRANCIS [*after a pause*]. Was there no more, Brother ? . . . Hadst thou written no more ?

LEO [*with an effort*]. There is more, Father ; but I cannot read it !

FRANCIS [*reaching up his hand for the MS.*]. Who was with thee just now ? I heard voices.

LEO. Brother Juniper.

FRANCIS. God did well when He made Brother Juniper.

[*So thinks LEO, but the word cannot find utterance.*
If thou art ever in doubt, Leo,—tell it to Brother Juniper : for God hath given him a simple heart. . . . Where is thy scrip ? [*LEO gives him the MS.*]. Nay ! it is written plain ; why couldst thou not read it ?

LEO [*with an effort*]. I will read it, Father.

[LEO *puts out his hand for the MS.* FRANCIS *retains it, sitting mazed in meditation.*

FRANCIS. Brother Leo . . . last night I saw one crucified, and bearing the pains of death—not for love, but for hate.

LEO. That was strange, Father.

FRANCIS. Yea, a great marvel : but strange are the ways of men. The face was a face I knew : one that I had loved well.

LEO. Who was that, Father ?

FRANCIS. Brother Sin.

[*With a quick instinctive gesture* LEO *crosses himself.*

LEO. What like was he, Father ?

FRANCIS. He is like a leper, Brother : separate and cut off from his own kind. He crieth, and none heareth ; he is athirst, yet will not drink ; he is in darkness, yet will not look on light. He hath need, and knoweth it not. The love of God vexeth him, for the love of God will not let him go.

[*During this recital* LEO'S *face shows an ever livelier emotion.*

Dost thou remember, Leo, how once thou didst wash the feet of a leper, because he so hated thee ?

LEO. Aye.

FRANCIS. So that, after, he hated thee no more.

LEO. That was long ago, Father. Now—*he* is in peace.

FRANCIS. Then I learned of thee, Leo. Then didst thou bring me nearer to Christ.

[LEO *bows his head ; his breast is shaken by sobs, but he makes no sound.*

So would I wash the feet of Brother Sin,—because he hateth me.

> [*There is a pause.* FRANCIS *sits lost in thought.* LEO *stands waiting ; his eyes are shut, as with a covert motion he beats upon his breast.*

Leo, wilt thou go for me to Father Minister Elias, and say that I, little Brother Francis, do ask of him forgiveness and blessing. Say that were I not lame, I would come to him myself.

LEO [*accepting an order whose meaning he cannot fathom*]. I will go, Father.

> [*Unseen by* FRANCIS *he pauses for a moment, as though about to throw himself at his feet, then goes quickly out.* FRANCIS *sits waiting : presently his eyes grow tranced.*

FRANCIS. Ah, Thou that lookest upon me through these eyes of hate, Lover of my life, depart not from me yet ! O Light, O Beauty, O Desire of mine eyes, out of the heart of this mine enemy come to me, that I with Thee, through him, may be made one ! Thee, whom I held bound, Thee will I release ; Thee, whom I feared, Thee will I trust. My Maker, my God, come down to me from Thy Cross, and be known to me—through the sins of men. This spear of doubt, these nails of fear, these thorns of envy, wherewith hate hath wounded Thee,—O Brother Sin, Brother Sin, turn not away—open thine eyes, that through them I may look on Him we have pierced !

LEO [*returning*]. He is not there, Father.

> [FRANCIS *stays tranced.* LEO *kneels before him.*

O Father, what dost thou see ?

FRANCIS [*become dimly aware of him*]. Brother

18

Leo, lay thy hand on me.

> [LEO, *approaching on his knees, lays his hands on the heart of* FRANCIS. *With bowed head and face half-averted, he waits fearfully till* FRANCIS *again speaks.*

Brother Leo, often with these hands thou hast done wrong, yet now they comfort me. Often with thine eyes thou hast been blind, yet in them I see light. Often with thy tongue thou hast denied thy Lord: yet never hath He denied me thee. Often hast thou forgotten God; yet thou dost remind me of Him.

LEO. Father, thou dost break my heart! Ah, go from me! Go from me!

FRANCIS [*in tender surprise*]. Brother Leo!

> [LEO *bows himself at the knees of* FRANCIS, *and breaks into passionate weeping.* FRANCIS *lays his hands on him.*

My son . . . what is thy trouble ? . . . Now, on holy obedience, I charge thee tell it me.

LEO. To be near thee, Father!

FRANCIS [*after a pause*]. Go from me, Leo . . . if thou wilt.

LEO. I would not, Father.

FRANCIS. Then come nearer to me. . . . Look on me! Lift up thy head! . . . O Brother—little sheep—is it not strange that we, children of Love, look upon each other thus through eyes of flesh ? For what parts us each from each—*that* we can see ; but what joins us we cannot see. Had we been blind, with no eyes to separate us, we should have been nearer—in our infirmity. But now, because face looketh upon face, we seem to be twain.

LEO. That is true, Father. As *thou* seest, I can-

19

not see. O Father Francis, where from my heart has gone the love of Christ ?

FRANCIS. Unto mine, Brother. For when He gave me thy love, He gave me His also. . . . Leo, give me thy pen. . . . And thy hand. . . . Now by thy hand I will write something. Shut thine eyes, little sheep . . . till I bid thee open them.

[*Guiding the hand of* LEO, FRANCIS *begins writing.*

Brother Pen goeth swiftly . . . this that we write pleaseth him. . . . Dost thou know what it is that we have written—thou, and I, and he ?

LEO. No, Father.

FRANCIS [*reading*]. ' The Lord bless thee and keep thee. The Lord make His face to shine upon thee.

[FRANCIS *slowly rises.* LEO *kneels.*

The Lord lift up the light of His countenance upon thee, and give thee peace. . . . Brother Leo, the Lord bless thee, as thou hast blest me.' [*He gives him the parchment.*] When thou art in trouble show this to Brother Sin.

LEO. Brother Sin !

FRANCIS. Do not be afraid of Brother Sin. He is a leper ; but when thou hast washed his feet, then shalt thou see . . . in them . . . the wounds of Christ. Yea, when for us Christ died—with Him also died—Brother Sin.

[LEO *rises to his feet with a face of ecstasy.*

LEO. Now am I made whole ! . . . Ah, Maker Christ ! Maker Christ !

[*He goes back to the Crucifix, draws away the curtain, and kneels.* FRANCIS, *seeing him rapt in prayer, turns softly, and with great pain hobbles back to his cell.*

20

KIND COMFORT

In the garden of St. Damien's, outside the walls of the Convent, under the rough wattled shelter that has been made for him, lies FRANCIS *in a sickness from which he will never recover. Feeble and suffering, he lies at the close of day, watching the moon-rise. From the valley below comes the sound of singing—too distant for the words to be heard. Presently the singing ceases for a while: there is silence;* FRANCIS *lies motionless; after a pause, he speaks.*

FRANCIS. Sister Night—pray for me ! . . . Sweet Sister Night . . . Oh, sweet comforting Sister Night, pray, pray for me—for I am broken !

[*Again distant singing is heard.* CLARE *enters.*

CLARE. Are you asleep, Little Father ?

FRANCIS. No, Sister.

CLARE. Nor wishing to sleep ?

FRANCIS. No, Sister. . . . Sister Night has come, but it is still early. . . . What is that singing ?

CLARE. 'Tis the wine-harvest, Little Father. They are singing the Vintage.

FRANCIS. Already finished ? Is it all over ?

CLARE. In the vineyards below, Brother. Other vineyards that see less of the sun are still waiting.

FRANCIS. Aye. Other vineyards that see less of the sun . . . are still waiting.

CLARE. Other things wait also, Little Father. The Sisters were asking to-day whether they might come and be with you for a while—since to-morrow you are leaving us.

FRANCIS. Yes, Sister, surely! But why had they to ask? Must they not be as welcome to me as I to them, that am their guest?

CLARE. Their Little Father, Brother.

FRANCIS. My Little Sisters, Mother. . . . Yes . . . ask them to come!

[CLARE *goes to call the* Sisters.

FRANCIS. Oh, Pain! Pain! Sister Pain! Be gentle to me for a while, Sister Pain!

[*The* Sisters *enter, a little timidly, fearful of disturbing him.* CLARE *follows, and stands closing the gate, as they advance.*

FRANCIS. Come, Sisters . . . come, come, come! How long have I not waited for you!

SISTER MONICA. We for you, Little Father.

FRANCIS. Nay, but I was here, as ye knew.

SISTER ANNA. Reverend Mother said that, if we came, we should talk too much.

FRANCIS. Did you, Sister?

CLARE. I did, Brother.

FRANCIS. Why?

CLARE. Because, surely, it is true. Under the Rule, we hold our tongues, and do well by it. But when the Rule lets us go, we talk too much, and talk foolishly.

FRANCIS. Sometimes, Sister, to talk foolishly gives comfort and refreshment—not only to our-

selves, but to others. . . . There is Brother
Juniper.

CLARE. Yes, Little Father—a good exception,
by God's mercy.

FRANCIS. No, Sister ; a *rule*—had we the mind
for it. Could we but all have followed *him*, what
a Brotherhood we should have been !

CLARE. A good Brotherhood, Little Father ;
but whither would he have guided us ?

FRANCIS. To ways of wisdom, which we have
missed, Sister. From none have I had better
guidance than from Brother Juniper. For often
has wisdom led me to foolishness, till from his
foolishness I have come back to wisdom. So,
Sisters—if Reverend Mother will allow—let us all
be foolish awhile. May we, Sister Mother ?

CLARE. They may be anything you like, Little
Father—you leading them.

FRANCIS. Then, Sisters, let us now look back
into our lives, and find which of us has been the
greatest fool, and has most thanked God for it.
For I think that that one of us will have been the
wisest.

SISTER ANNA. How—'look into our lives,' Father?

FRANCIS. By telling, each one, something about
yourselves—which you once did, and which others
thought foolish, but which to you seemed good—
and still does so. Thus, from each other, shall
we learn wisdom. . . . [*A pause.*] Come ! Have
you all been so wise in your lives, that you have
nothing foolish to tell ?

SISTER MONICA. Too much to hide, Father.

FRANCIS. Nay, but that is foolishness of another

kind. The foolishness we are to hear about is the foolishness which still seems good to you. . . . Sister Zarepha, you are laughing.

SISTER ZAREPHA. Yes, Little Father.

FRANCIS. Tell us, then.

SISTER ZAREPHA. But truly, in the telling, Father, 'twill seem so foolish !

FRANCIS. All the better, Sister. . . . Come !

SISTER ZAREPHA. Well, then, here's to begin. 'Twas when I was but young—before I had come here to a life of religion. My mother used often to beat me ; doubt not but I deserved it.

FRANCIS. We doubt not, Sister.

SISTER ZAREPHA. Aye : for anything she thought to be wrong, short and sharp was her way with me ! I didn't like it ; and that was foolish of me, wasn't it, Father ?

FRANCIS. Surely ; since liking would have so much eased it for thee.

SISTER ZAREPHA. But sometimes I did a thing she did not find out, so did not beat me for it : but that not often. One day I had done a great sin—oh, a very great sin ! Am I to tell what the sin was, Father ?

FRANCIS. No, Sister.

SISTER ZAREPHA. Well, that sin—the biggest I'd ever done—she didn't find out. So it was on my mind I had not got the beating for it I deserved. And that so frightened me, Father, that one day I fell to, and began beating myself. My mother came in and caught me at it. ' Are you mad, Child ? ' says she. ' No, Mother,' said I. ' I'm only mothering myself for a thing I ought not to

have done.' But that didn't a bit please her.
'I'll mother you,' she said, 'when you need
mothering! What was it you were beating yourself for?' I wouldn't tell her; and for that she
beat me far worse than she'd ever beaten me
before. Well, Father, that didn't seem fair,
somehow, to be beaten twice over for the same
thing—though a great sin it was that I'm not
to tell you. So I just ran away; and then one
day it came to me how foolish it was to mind
being beaten twice over for a sin I'd done, when
Our Lord was so much worse beaten for sins He'd
never done. And 'twas that foolishness, and the
thought it gave me, brought me here, Father.
And Reverend Mother knows what the sin was—
though I'm not to tell it to the rest of you.

CLARE. No, Sister; you have told quite enough.
And there is Sister Angela looking so foolish that
I think she also has something to tell.

FRANCIS. Have you, Sister?

SISTER ANGELA. Yes, Little Father; and a foolish
story it must be; for 'twas an ass herself was
the cause of it, as you shall now hear. One day,
as I passed a stable-yard, an ass came running to
the gate, braying to be let out; and for good
reason—her foal having been taken from her only
that day. So there we were—she one side of the
gate, and I the other; and she looking at me with
eyes so plain I could not mistake. . . . Now that
day I had prayed, saying, 'Lord, let me not go my
own way, but *Thy* way. Show it me, this day;
and wheresoever it takes me, there will I go.' So,
seeing the ass, I thought of our dear Lord riding

to Jerusalem; and it seemed to me that I could do no better than get on the back of the ass, and let her take me as God Himself willed it. So I did—climbing the gate first, then opening it, then mounting quick as she passed through. Five miles she ran, Father, with me riding her; and surely God's Hand must have been on her, for that was what brought me here. Outside, against the garden-wall she threw me, breaking my leg, and my head also; and there the Reverend Mother came out and found me. So—from doing a foolish thing—I stayed to do a wise one.

SISTER URSULA. Aye, it's true, Father. If sometimes we weren't foolish, we'd never learn to be wise. The foolishest thing I ever did in my life taught *me*—thank God for it!

FRANCIS. Yes, Sister? What foolishest thing was that?

SISTER URSULA. Hankering after what wasn't mine, Father. One day I found a purse of gold lying in the road, and no one in sight that it could belong to. I said to myself, ' This is mine, as much as it's anyone's that I know; yet not mine truly. How, then, shall I know if it be God's will that I keep it as mine? ' I did this: I waited till it was dark; then I went out in my father's field and buried it. ' And if,' said I, ' I can find it again, then 'twill be God's will that I keep it. . . . And if I do not find it, then 'twill *not* be His will.' I never found it again, Father.

FRANCIS. And which was the foolish thing, Sister—the finding, or the losing?

SISTER URSULA. Both, Little Father: for, having

the gold, yet not having the use of it—knowing it to be safe, yet unable to find it—I learned soon to care less for it—finding I could as well do without. And 'twas strange how, telling no one—(for had I told others, they might have searched and found it)—I still felt it to be mine, while daily my want for it grew less; till at last it seemed no longer to mean anything to me. So one day, having lost all wish to possess that which stayed hid, I let thought of it go, and came here; and here have been these twelve years, Father, made wise by that foolishness.

FRANCIS. And did you tell no one of the gold, Sister, that you had ceased caring for?

SISTER URSULA. No indeed, Father. But the very day I came away—by chance—digging, my old Dad found it. And that was a God's showing, wasn't it, Father?

FRANCIS. It may have been, Sister. Did the finding of it make *him* happy?

SISTER URSULA. No, Father; for two days later, others, that had heard tell of it, came by night and robbed him. It broke his heart for him, that did; for which—since it was my doing—I ought now to be sorry. Aye; though my foolishness helped *me*, it did not help *him*: God rest him to peace!

FRANCIS. Who knows, Sister? There be some hearts which needs must be broken in this world, so that they may get mended in Heaven. By my folly I broke my Father's heart; yet was it good for him.

THE SISTERS. By your folly, Little Father? What folly?

FRANCIS. This life that I have lived, Sister, since

I left that which he planned for me. He planned that I should be rich : I that I would be poor. He that I should marry Wealth, and get sons and daughters : I that I would wed Poverty, and have only brothers and sisters.

CLARE. And yet be the Father of them.

FRANCIS. Yes, Sister. But that was God's doing, not mine. And how I came to have so many, truly, I know not ! Aye, Folly has been kind to me ! And the hearts that my foolishness has broken, God's wisdom shall mend. Let us all pray, Little Sisters, that God will show us in what ways to be foolish, and in what ways to be wise, the better to serve Him. Yet shall we ever serve Him more truly and safely knowing ourselves fools than believing ourselves wise. 'Tis a great mercy, Sisters, how God has found a use for fools ; for had He not done so, few be they that could have had hope of salvation.

[*Enter the* LAY SISTER.

LAY SISTER. Reverend Mother, one of the Brothers is at the gate, asking for the Little Father.

CLARE. Bring him in, Sister.

[*She goes, and returns, followed by* JUNIPER. Brother Juniper !

JUNIPER. What, all of ye here together ? Ye look like a hatch of chickens, all sitting there, so close under each other's feathers and the Little Father's, that it's hard to tell which is which of you.

FRANCIS. And am I the cock or the hen, Juniper ?

JUNIPER. You're the cock *and* the hen. Ye

don't crow and ye don't cackle ; but ye *do* cluck, Father. Down there by the gate waiting, I heard you. What was it all about, Father ?

FRANCIS. Fools, Juniper ; and foolishness.

JUNIPER. God save you from both, Father !

FRANCIS. Indeed no, Juniper. For had He done so, you would not be here now.

JUNIPER [*accommodatingly*]. Oh ? Shall I go away, Father ?

FRANCIS. You shall not, Juniper. But you, also, shall now answer the question that has been concerning us. . . . What is the best foolish thing that you have ever done in your life, Juniper ? Think well !

JUNIPER. Sure, that's easy enough to answer, Father dear, without thinking ! Being born was the best foolish thing that ever *I* did.

FRANCIS. Why best, Juniper ? And why foolish ?

JUNIPER. Why, surely for a born fool to be born *must* be foolish. But if I *hadn't* been born, I wouldn't have found you, Father.

FRANCIS. Wouldn't have found God, Brother.

JUNIPER. I'd never have found God but for you, Father dear.

FRANCIS. God would have found thee, Brother. Aye, even hadst thou been blind, He would have had eyes for thee. And this truth have I learned for myself, first from thee, and through thee from others, Juniper : that howsoever we lose God in this beautiful world of His making, still He finds us again ; and often by the help of fools.

[*From within the Convent a bell starts ringing.*

CLARE. That is the bell, Father. We must go now, and leave you. Your blessing, Father.

FRANCIS. God rest you to peace, Sisters.

THE SISTERS [*with variations*]. God rest you, Little Father, and give you good sleep.[1]

[CLARE *gives the* Lay Sister *the keys.*

FRANCIS. Is it now that you must lock up the gate for the night, Sister?

CLARE. That is the Rule, Father. Brother Juniper, come round to the gate, and get the Little Father his broth, which now will be ready for him. Goodnight, Father.

FRANCIS. Good-night, Sister. God give you rest.

[*The* Sisters *have gone.* CLARE *and* JUNIPER *follow.* FRANCIS *is left alone. The moon has now risen high and bright, and shines in under the wattled shelter, but only on his hands, not on his face. Under the shadow one hears a sharp catch of breath.*

FRANCIS. Oh, Pain! Gentle Sister Pain, hast thou come back to me? Welcome, welcome, Sister Pain.

[JUNIPER *returns with the broth; and offers it to* FRANCIS.

JUNIPER. Here is your broth, Father, and some bread to go with it.

FRANCIS. Drink it for me, Juniper, for *I* cannot.

JUNIPER. Nay, but 'twas made for *you*, Father.

FRANCIS. I cannot, Brother; to-night I cannot! Set it down—set it down, Juniper!

---

[1] *I.e.* 'God give you good sleep, Little Father,' or 'God rest you to sleep, Little Father,' or 'God rest and give you good sleep, Little Father,' etc.

JUNIPER. If you won't eat or drink, then, Father, now you must sleep.

FRANCIS. Aye, if I can, Juniper.

JUNIPER. If you can't, then I must make you.

FRANCIS. Aye, make me, if you can !

JUNIPER. On holy obedience, Father dear, you are to sleep.

FRANCIS. Pray for me, Juniper : then, God helping me, I will.

JUNIPER. Holy Jesus, Maker and Lover of men, give sleep to the Little Father this night. Comfort and be kind to him. Take away from him all pain, all sorrow, all doubt, all trouble of mind and body, all care and unrest, all sickness ; and if he be in pain now, let me bear it for him, and I will be thankful. Amen. . . . To Thy taking, to Thy keeping ; for making, for reaping ; for mending or breaking, watching or sleeping, let all bodies and souls be thine, at the last Day's waking. Amen. . . .

    [*He pauses, and bends over to look at* FRANCIS.
Are you asleep, Father ?

    [*There is no answer. From the tree overhead
    comes the slow soft hoot of an owl.*

Hush, hush, Sister ! . . . The Little Father's asleep. Don't wake him.

    [*Again, disregarding* JUNIPER'S *petition, comes
    the hoot of the owl, soft and prolonged. But
    *FRANCIS *does not wake.*

CURTAIN

MAKERS OF MIRACLE

In the Community room, on a portable bed in one corner of it, lies FRANCIS. Bandaged feet and hands, covering the marks of the stigmata, give a date not far from the end. On the other side of the room is an open hearth, with a fire on it; round about it are a bench and a few stools. From a door at the back JUNIPER looks in, and with rapt reverence stands watching, till FRANCIS, becoming aware, opens eyes at him.

FRANCIS. Juniper.

JUNIPER. Yes, Father?

FRANCIS. Come and talk to me.

JUNIPER. What about, Father?

FRANCIS. Life, Brother.

JUNIPER. That's too big a bite for *my* wits, Father. Life, eh? Which life, then? If it's this, ye mean—God keep you in it, is all *I* pray. But if I was to start talking to ye about Heaven now——

FRANCIS. Yes, Brother?

JUNIPER. I should put my foot in it, so you'd never get there.

FRANCIS. Your foot is in it already, Brother.

33

JUNIPER. Not my head, though ! And as I can't talk on my toes, there 's no telling ye about it with them. Are you better, Father dear ?

FRANCIS. I shall be, Juniper, when you have talked to me.

JUNIPER. Sure, Father, what you take to be a cure, others would want to die of.

FRANCIS. So they might, Juniper. God's ways are wonderful. But we have only to love them well enough, and we shall all die—of happiness.

JUNIPER. But I want to keep you alive, Father ! Must that make you miserable ?

FRANCIS. No, Brother. One cannot be miserable with you.

JUNIPER. Yet we are all miserable sinners, Father.

FRANCIS. Without knowing it, God being merciful.   [*He stops ; pain takes hold of him.*

JUNIPER. Have you a bad pain, Father ?

FRANCIS. Pain is good, Brother ; when it has company. . . . Talk, Juniper !

[*But the pain that* FRANCIS *is bearing is too evident for* JUNIPER *to find talk easy ; he can only ' make conversation.'*

JUNIPER. It 's snowing, Father.

FRANCIS. Yes ?

JUNIPER. I came through it ; had my feet in it ; when I looked back, there were the marks how I 'd come, all the way. You could count every step— though 'twas getting dark then. . . . I hope God doesn't remember to count all our sins that way !

FRANCIS. No, Brother, no. He does not.

JUNIPER. If He did, I'd have to start walking on my head.

FRANCIS. Why, Brother ?

JUNIPER. Because—though my sins have got two feet under 'em—'twould be only one head : so that 'd halve the track of 'em, at any rate. . . . What are you laughing at, Father dear ?

FRANCIS. At you, Juniper.

JUNIPER. Has it cured the pain ?

FRANCIS. Yes, Brother. Go on.

JUNIPER. So while I was looking back to see the way I 'd come, I saw something else. . . . Listen, Father ! There, alongside in the snow, tripping the same way, little feet, little feet—oh ! ever so little : smaller than any bird's—so small, they made me afraid, Father.

FRANCIS. Of what, Brother ?

JUNIPER. Sure, of myself : for being so much bigger, yet no better.

FRANCIS. Than what ?

JUNIPER. 'Twas a mouse, Father !

[*On this important discovery* JUNIPER *makes a pause, that* FRANCIS *may feel the thrill of it.*

FRANCIS. Yes ?

JUNIPER. And presently, just ahead of me, I saw her running, running for her life !

FRANCIS. Yes ?

JUNIPER. So I followed her.

FRANCIS. To save it ?

JUNIPER. She saved it for herself, Father. In she ran, under the gate, into the garden, with me after her. Just in time I looked over ; and there she was going down into the snow, some little way of her own, by where the parsley used to grow.

FRANCIS. Where it is growing still, Brother. For though Sister Snow is cold in her bed, others she keeps in life and gives warmth to.

JUNIPER. Sure, I never thought of it!

FRANCIS. So there be three sisters in one bed: Sister Snow, Sister Parsley, and Sister Mouse.

JUNIPER. Doing what, Father?

FRANCIS. I don't know, Juniper: finding life in the way God meant them to.

JUNIPER. Does a mouse, when it can't get meal, or grain, eat parsley, do you think, Father?

FRANCIS. It may, Juniper; for parsley is good eating, so good that often before now I have eaten more of it than was wise.

JUNIPER. Would parsley make *me* wise, Father?

FRANCIS. No, Brother.

JUNIPER. Sure, then, I needn't be afraid of it.

FRANCIS. Be afraid of nothing, Juniper—— Where are you going?

JUNIPER. There's a pot on, Father. I'm making you some broth. And while I'm gone, Brother Angelo and Brother Jerome, and the new Brother you haven't seen yet, shall come in and look after you. They're in the kitchen now warming themselves.

FRANCIS. I would rather be alone, Juniper.

JUNIPER. Yes, Father; but you mayn't be. It's against orders. But they shan't talk to you, Father: and don't you talk to them. You've talked enough.

FRANCIS. Is it on holy obedience, Juniper, that I am not to talk?

JUNIPER. It's on holy obedience that you talk when you want to talk, and not when any one else wants you. I'll tell them you are just off to sleep; and you won't make me be telling a lie, will you, Father?

FRANCIS. I won't make you do anything, Juniper, that isn't in you to do.

JUNIPER. Then you're asleep, aren't you, Father?

FRANCIS [*drowsily*]. Yes, Brother . . . yes.

[JUNIPER *gives a sigh of satisfaction; then, with a hushing sound, as a mother over the cradle of her child, stands watching. Presently reverent awe takes hold of him; he is silent a while, then speaks.*

JUNIPER. O Lord, keep your holy eyes on him! When he's asleep, doesn't he look beautiful? Like a well of deep water, and the moon shining in it so clear!   [*He goes softly out.*

FRANCIS [*murmuring softly to himself*].

    Sister Mouse
    Has her house
    Down below
    In the snow.
    Where the parsley bed
    Is spread;—
    Nothing there to show—
    Sister Mouse
    Has her house
    Down below.

[JUNIPER *re-enters, accompanied by* JEROME, ANGELO, *and the* NOVICE.

JUNIPER. Yes, he's asleep; I've his own word

for it ; so you 're not to talk to him ! Go, and sit over there and talk to yourselves—quietly, so you don't wake him. And if he talks to you, in his sleep, give him the short answer for it, and tell him I say he 's not to be awake till his broth 's ready for him. [*He goes out.*

NOVICE. Which of us is that, Brothers ?

JEROME. Brother Juniper.

ANGELO. He is very foolish and ignorant.

JEROME. But the little Father has found a use for him.

ANGELO. And when he is ill he attends on him.

NOVICE. The little Father ! oh, may I go and look at him ?

ANGELO. He lies there, Brother.

JEROME. Go reverently.

ANGELO. Remembering the miracle.

JEROME. His whole life is now a miracle.

ANGELO. Aye, surely.

NOVICE. He is asleep.

ANGELO. No, Brother ; not asleep. He is in a trance, or having a vision.

NOVICE. Does he tell you his visions ?

ANGELO. Everything that he says now we write down.

JEROME. The Father Minister has commanded it.

NOVICE. Why, Brother ?

ANGELO. Because all that he says now is holy, and full of mystery, and comes from God.

JEROME. For our instruction—and to keep us from the world. You have your tablets, Brother Angelo ?

ANGELO. Of course, Brother.

JEROME. Also the Father Minister has ordered that he shall never be left alone, lest anything he say be unrecorded.

ANGELO. Which is why I am here now with my tablets.

NOVICE. Are you always able to understand, or to interpret what he says, Brother ?

JEROME. No, Brother : but when we do not, the Father Minister understands it for us.

ANGELO. That is why he has ordered us to write everything down as soon as it is uttered.

NOVICE. What you tell me is very wonderful, Brothers. It frightens me.

ANGELO. We also are full of holy fear, Brother.

[*The sound of a sigh came from the bed.*

JEROME. Hush ! Did he speak ?

[*They rise from their seats, and stand looking toward* FRANCIS ; *and are so standing, expectantly, when* JUNIPER *re-enters.*

JUNIPER. Are you doing as I told you, now ? Not waking him to have him talk to you ?

[ANGELO *puts finger on lip ;* JEROME *follows suit. The* Novice *catches the infection and does likewise. Their warning sibilation sounds in chorus.*

JUNIPER. Keep as ye are, then ! His broth is almost ready for him. [*He goes out.*

NOVICE [*a little crestfallen*]. So ?—He does take *food*, then, sometimes ?

ANGELO. Only on holy obedience, Brother, and because Father Minister commands it. Had he his own choice, I think he would eat nothing—living only on things spiritual.

ANGELO. How he lives, even now, is a great mystery.

JEROME. A great miracle.

[*Softly from the bed,* FRANCIS *lifts an arm ; he opens his eyes, and to the holy agitation of the three listeners begins to speak. They all go upon their knees.* ANGELO *gets out his tablets and starts writing.*

FRANCIS. Sister Mouse
　　　　Has her house
　　　　Down below
　　　　In the snow.
　　　　Softly, softly, softly tread !
　　　　Where the parsley bed
　　　　Is spread,—
　　　　Nothing but her feet to show,—
　　　　Sister Mouse
　　　　Has her house
　　　　Down below.

[*A short silence follows.*

JEROME. Have you written it, Brother ?

ANGELO [*busy writing*]. Sh !

[*They watch him while he finishes.*

JEROME. What—what does it mean ?

ANGELO. We must be humble, Brother, and patient. Father Elias will tell us what it means.

JEROME. ' Sister Mouse, has her house ' : that must mean the soul and the body, surely !—but why in the snow ?

ANGELO. I have it all written down, Brother. Father Elias will explain.

NOVICE. Sh! See!

> [FRANCIS *slightly raises himself.*

JEROME. He is awake. He has heard us.

FRANCIS. Who is there?

ANGELO [*rising*]. There are three of us, little Father. I am Brother Angelo; this is Brother Jerome; and here is the new Brother just come.

> [*The* Novice *rises, advances, and kneels.*

FRANCIS. God bless thee, little new Brother, and give thee peace! 'Tis a cold night: you have come through the snow?

NOVICE. Yes, Father.

FRANCIS. Sit, and warm yourself. . . . Brother Angelo?

ANGELO. Yes, Father?

> [*He hands his tablets to* JEROME. JEROME *writes.*

FRANCIS. Brother Juniper is making a broth for me. Go into the garden, get some parsley, take it, and tell him to put it in the broth, so as to flavour it.

ANGELO. But, little Father, the garden has hardly any parsley in it; and only in one place, which, now that it is dark, I shall not be able to find.

FRANCIS. But go and try, Brother.

JEROME. Indeed, Father, I have tried already only to-day. Brother Rufus sent me for it; but there was so much snow I could not find where it grew.

FRANCIS. Try again, Brother.

JEROME. But now, Father, it is snowing again, so that it lies deeper. And it is dark, also.

FRANCIS. Yes; but try, Brother.

> [ANGELO *and* JEROME *look at each other in perplexity. The tablets are neglected.*

ANGELO. Father, we cannot quite understand. We do not think that you mean parsley. What do you mean ?

FRANCIS. I mean—parsley, Brother.

ANGELO. Perhaps you had better go, Brother. Perhaps, when you fail to find any, his meaning will be revealed to us.

FRANCIS. Yes, do go, Brother !   [JEROME *goes*.

ANGELO. I am afraid he will be a long time, Father.

FRANCIS. I can wait, Brother.

ANGELO. And if he cannot find any, Father ?

FRANCIS. Then I can have it some other day.

[*Re-enter* JUNIPER.

JUNIPER. Ah ! There you are awake again ! Father dear, would you like a bit of parsley put into your broth, so as to flavour it ?

FRANCIS. Yes, Brother.

JUNIPER. D'you think one of the Brothers could go, then, and get it for me ?

FRANCIS. I think he could, Brother.

JUNIPER. And will one of you, then ?

FRANCIS. One of them has gone, Brother.   I sent him.

JUNIPER. Oh, that was thoughtful of ye, now ! And it means you 'd got a fancy for it, doesn't it ?

FRANCIS. Yes, Brother.

JUNIPER. And that you 're going to enjoy eating it !

FRANCIS. Yes, Brother.

JUNIPER. The Lord be praised !   Ah, He knows how to make you better, doesn't He ?—when He 's got Juniper to help Him do it.

FRANCIS. Yes, Brother.

[*This conversation about things material has not been at all to the liking of* BROTHER ANGELO, *who now summons* JUNIPER, *to warn him of the mistake he is making.*

ANGELO. Brother . . . Brother Juniper!

JUNIPER [*crossing to the call*]. Aye ?

ANGELO. I charge you, Brother, not to talk so much. Here, while you were away, something has been happening.

JUNIPER. Eh ? What was it, then ?

ANGELO. I cannot explain, Brother. It is still a mystery. When Brother Jerome returns, what it means may be revealed to us.

NOVICE. The little Father has had a vision, Brother.

JUNIPER. What, another ? He gets more than is good for him, I 'm thinking.

NOVICE. Saying strange things——

ANGELO. And laying on us a strange command, which we could not understand—but yet have obeyed.

[*Behind their backs, meanwhile,* BROTHER JEROME *has returned ; he approaches the bed.*

JEROME. Here it is, little Father !

JUNIPER. Why, he 's been and fetched us the parsley !

ANGELO. Oh, wonder ! Oh, miracle !

FRANCIS. So : you found it, Brother ?

JEROME. Yes. I went, Father, even as you told me, though doubting much—for it was almost dark. And there, under the wall where the snow lay light, I put down my hand—so ; and feeling about where it was lightest, I found this, Father. Picking it,

I did not know what it was ; but when I brought it to the light, then I saw that, though much of it was grass, there was parsley in it too—a very little.

JUNIPER. Eh, but it 's enough ! So now, Father, you 'll have your broth flavoured just as you wanted it—the Lord be praised !

[*He takes it, and runs out.*

ANGELO. Little Father, forgive our lack of faith ! Thou hast done a wonder !

FRANCIS. O Brothers, when I ask for something to be done, I wish you would not make me say it —so often !

[FRANCIS *shuts his eyes again. Another* Brother *enters, and, while* ANGELO *draws* JEROME *mysteriously aside for the communication of his awe-struck mind, stands listening.*

ANGELO. So now it is revealed to us ! This he did to try our faith ; and to confirm it hath wrought miracle !

FRANCIS [*almost in a whisper*].

Sister Mouse
Has her house
In the snow. . . .
There, down below,
Parsleys grow.

[*The* Brothers, *crossing themselves, hold their breath and wait for more, till continued silence tells them that, for the moment, revelation is over.*

JEROME. Write it down, Brother ! Write it down !

[ANGELO *brings out his tablets ; then, catching sight of the newly arrived* Brother, *stops to give him an errand.*

44

ANGELO. Go, Brother, quickly : tell Father Minister I have holy news for him.

        [*The* Brother *scutters out in haste.*

FRANCIS. Softly, softly, softly tread !
        Where the parsley-bed
        Is spread,
            In the snow,
            Nothing but her feet to show !

JEROME. Did you hear that, Brother ?—Write it down !

    [*The* Brother *re-enters, still on the scutter with excitement.*

BROTHER. I 've told him ; I 've told all of them ! Father Minister is coming, Brother.

    [FATHER ELIAS *enters, followed hurriedly at intervals by other* Brothers, *who all gather round to listen. At the entrance of* ELIAS, ANGELO *and those with him rise up in meek reverence.*

ELIAS. Yes, Brother ?

ANGELO. Father Minister, the little Father has been speaking again.

ELIAS. Well, Brother ?

ANGELO. In words we could not understand— that seemed mystery.

ELIAS. Go on, Brother !

ANGELO. Then, after having spoken, he gave command that brought . . . wonder !

ELIAS. Give me your report, Brother, quickly. Have you it written ?

ANGELO. I was still writing it when you came, Father.

ELIAS. Report what you have heard ; and let the writing be afterwards.

ANGELO [*crossing himself*]. In nomine Patris, et Filii, et Spiritus Sancti. . . . First he spoke in parable, Father; not to us sitting here, but as though he beheld it above his head, in a vision.

[*Awe begins to descend on the listening community; one by one they cross themselves.*

I wrote down the words, Father.

ELIAS. Read them!

ANGELO. Sister Mouse
   Has her house
   Down below
   In the snow. . . .

[*He looks at* FATHER MINISTER *to gather its effect on him.*

What does that mean, Father?

JEROME. Does it mean the soul and the body, Father?

BROTHER. Or does the mouse mean a nibbling pain, Father?

ELIAS. Continue, Brother. We will consider what it means afterwards.

ANGELO. Then, Father, he spoke of parsley; and surely that seemed a great mystery, that he should speak of parsley at such a time, so near to his dying, and he so holy! We could not understand what it meant, Father.

JEROME. Does the parsley mean the Blessed Sacrament, do you think, Father?

ELIAS. Continue, Brother.

ANGELO. Then, Father, came the marvel. He told one of us, on holy obedience, to go and fetch it for him.

ELIAS. Fetch what, Brother?

ANGELO. The parsley, Father. But I said that in the dark, and the deep snow, only by miracle could one find any. But he said one of us was to go instantly.

JEROME. He said that three times, Father.

ELIAS. Yes?

ANGELO. So Brother Jerome went. And all the time Brother Jerome was gone, there was light in his eyes, Father, like the lamp burning before the altar of the Blessed Sacrament. We were very much afraid, Father.

[*The awe-struck interest of the listening* Brothers *has now become intense. Only* ELIAS *remains unmoved.*

ELIAS. Continue, Brother.

ANGELO. So Brother Jerome went, Father; and the night was so dark he could not see his own hand even, nor where his feet were taking him. But no sooner had he entered the garden (for it was to the garden the little Father had told him to go; and 'tis marvel how he got there!) . . . there, under the wall, on the snow lay a light!

[*He looks at* JEROME *for confirmation.*

JEROME. 'Twas so, Father.

ANGELO. And just there, where the light most shone . . . sent by the little Father, to show him the way . . . he put out his hand and took up what first came to it. What had come to his hand he did not know till he lifted it to the light. And the light showed that it was parsley, Father!

[*A breath of wonder escapes from the listening* Brothers; *and in a devoutly receptive atmosphere the inspired narrative goes on.*

47

JEROME. Which I could never have found of myself, Father : no, Father !

ANGELO. And then, Father, when he had brought it back rejoicing, and showed it to him, the little Father said : [*he searches his tablets*] I haven't yet got it written, Father.

ELIAS. Said ?

ANGELO. 'So in faith you found it, Brother ? ' And he said, ' Yes, Father : but first I doubted.' Then the little Father said, ' O Brothers, sheep of my flock, doubt nothing ! Whatever I tell you to do, on holy obedience, do it instantly.' Then did we know, Father, why he had sent for the parsley —so that he might teach us by miracle to have faith and to be obedient.

ELIAS. Anything more, Brother ?

ANGELO. Yes, Father. After Brother Juniper had taken the parsley to put in the broth which he is making, presently we heard the little Father saying again the same words :

> Sister Mouse
> Has her house
> In the snow.
> There—down below—
> Parsleys grow. . . .

ELIAS. What then, Brother ?

ANGELO. Then we all crossed ourselves, Father, and waited, praying. And then, just before you came, the little Father said . . . Brother Jerome, you heard—what did he say ?

[*As* JUNIPER *enters, carrying the steaming broth, from the bed behind comes a voice.*

FRANCIS. The little Father said ' Ba-a-a ! '

[*They all turn and look ; but apparently* FRANCIS *is only talking in his sleep, or in a trance, or is having a vision. The voice of the bewildered* JUNIPER *breaks the silence.*

JUNIPER. What have ye all been doing to him, making a sheep of him ?

JEROME [*to* ANGELO]. Write it down, Brother ! Write it down !

CURTAIN

THE ORDER OF RELEASE

It is morning ; the sun shines upon the wall of the Convent of St. Damien's, in the centre of which stands a door, the upper part of it a grille. Inside, a Lay-sister is seen sweeping. Immediately above the door is a window all bars, with inner shutters, which, being part open, let out from within the sound of the Sisters of the Community singing their Office. JUNIPER *enters, carrying a large basket laden with eatables. With a heavy sigh he sets it down before the door, and seats himself dejectedly on a stone bench by the side of it. The singing catches his melancholy attention; he raises his head to listen, but finds no cheer in it. Presently he sights a wood-louse crossing the path in front of him. That's better—here is life that he can talk to.*

JUNIPER. Aye ; go your way, little sister, go your way ! You 've the legs for it—more than I have ; sixteen to my two ! You 'll die a good death before I do—the Lord helping you. And if anybody finds you good to eat, you 'll be more use in this world than ever I 'll be ! [*With a sigh he returns to silent meditation.*]

[*At this point the* Lay-sister *opens one half of the door inwards, on the side away from where* JUNIPER *is seated, and begins to sweep out the*

51

refuse. As she does so, she sights the basket, lays by her broom, and comes out to inspect. Then she sees JUNIPER, *but—his face being covered by his hood—is not quite sure of him.*

LAY-SISTER. Brother; Brother Juniper, is that you?

JUNIPER [*melancholy of tone*]. Aye.

LAY-SISTER. What brings you here, so early?

JUNIPER. Yon thing without legs asked me to carry it. In there is food for you.

LAY-SISTER. God reward your charity, Brother!

JUNIPER. It 's not mine.

LAY-SISTER. But you brought it.

JUNIPER. As I was told. There 's no charity in that. You 've just got to.

LAY-SISTER. Who was it told you, Brother?

JUNIPER. Nobody *you* know. But one that you do, told *him*, maybe. It 's what 's left over from last night, that they didn't eat at the Bishop's table. ' You 're to take that down to the little Sisters, by the Bishop's orders,' he says. So if it 's the Bishop's orders, it 's not for us to doubt but it 's God's orders too. So you can thank Him for it. And if you thank Him, and He didn't, He 'll forgive you, maybe.

[*All this is said so cheerlessly and unlike himself to those who know him, that the* Sister's *attention becomes solicitude.*

LAY-SISTER. Brother . . . what is the matter?

JUNIPER. All the world 's the matter! . . . And yet God made it: though, by the look of it, you 'd never think so. Eh! If it wasn't for the little Father I 'd have no faith in me left!

LAY-SISTER. How is the little Father?

JUNIPER. If you 'll fetch Sister Clare, you 'll save me telling it twice.   Where is she ?

LAY-SISTER. With all the others up there, saying the office.

JUNIPER. Tell 'em, when they 've done, I 've got news for 'em : something that wants more praying to put it right than I can do.

LAY-SISTER. I think they *have* finished, Brother ; I don't hear them now.

[*Indeed the morning office is already over ; and* SISTER CLARE, *passing the window, followed by others, stops at sound of voices below and looks out.*

JUNIPER [*meditatively*]. No : but there 's a lot that goes on in the world that we can't hear—ever. Yet it goes on, Sister.   Twenty-three years ago, *here 's* where I first set eyes on him.

LAY-SISTER. Who ?

JUNIPER. The little Father. . . . He was young, then, and beautiful like an angel ! . . . He wasn't in pain then—nor hadn't any sorrow—none that mattered.   He was building : two others with him. 'Twas then I came ; and Brother Silvestro— a priest he was then, and rich ; and Sister Gia- comina, she came too.   I wish she 'd come now, Sister !   That day, I remember, she said a thing— —made the little Father so happy—that he just stood there, where you are now, Sister—saying it, over and over to himself again : he so full of it !

LAY-SISTER. Saying what ?

JUNIPER. ' All the world is a-building !   All the world is a-building ! ' . . . And it seemed true then. [*He sighs heavily.*

CLARE. It is true still, Brother.

JUNIPER [*looking up*]. What ? Were you there listening, Sister dear ? True is it ? Where do you get that from, now ?

CLARE. From the world, Brother. God is in it, making us grow with all the rest of it.

JUNIPER. O Sister ! dear Sister Clare, come down, then, and talk to me ! It 's you I 've been wanting, that 's got the sense and the understanding to make me sure again of things I can't be sure of myself.

CLARE. I am coming, Brother.

[*She disappears from the window.*

JUNIPER [*shaking his head*]. Eh, but she knows ; she knows ! You can tell it by her voice. . . . And there 's the sun goes on shining—right into my eyes . . . not into my heart, though. My heart hasn't got eyes left to see it now.

CLARE [*appearing at the gate*]. The little Father, Brother ; how is he ?

[JUNIPER *makes a forlorn gesture, turns his face to the wall, and weeps. The* LAY-*sister, awaiting orders, shows the basket to* SISTER CLARE.

Take it in, Sister ; and when you have emptied it, bring it back with you. Then, go down into the garden and pick a bunch of lavender —for all of us : from the bush nearest the gate, Sister.

[*The* LAY-*sister, with a motion of obedience, goes in, carrying the basket.* SISTER CLARE *stands watching* JUNIPER.

The little Father does not weep, Brother. So neither must we.

JUNIPER [*struggling to express himself*]. O Sister, it's not because he's dying that I've lost myself. It's the way they're making him die is what breaks my heart. Sister, they are killing him !

CLARE. Where is he, Brother ? Two days ago we heard he had returned—not to Portiuncula, but to Assisi.

JUNIPER. Yes : he's at the Bishop's palace, Sister. And the citizens have put a guard round him.

CLARE. A guard ? Why, Brother ?

JUNIPER. So that he mayn't get out : so they shan't take him away ! He's got to stay in Assisi, they say—till he dies there.

CLARE. And our little Father : what does he say ?

JUNIPER. They don't let him say anything— that they'll give any heed to. He wants to be down at Portiuncula—for the end, Sister ; so as to be where he first made us be Brothers. And they won't let him !

CLARE. Doubt not, Brother, if it be God's will, the little Father will find a way to it.

JUNIPER. Yes, Sister : but they are making it hard for him.

CLARE. He never wanted things to be easy, Brother.

JUNIPER. No, Sister dear . . . but I'm not happy about him ; nor he's not happy about himself, either. The way they've got hold of him—it's like the Day of Judgment ; and them with a pair of scales, all so terribly holy, weighing the pieces of him. And there they sit, like a row of corpse-lights, watching him, and one of them with a big extinguisher, holding it over his head, ready to come down on him, and pinch him out the shape they want him to be.

CLARE. What shape, Brother ?

JUNIPER. They are breaking him to bits, to make a miracle of him ! It 's just this, Sister [*he breaks into weeping*], it 's just this : they want him dead and gone to his glory, more than they want him alive !

CLARE. He wants that himself, Brother.

JUNIPER. He has the right to want it : they haven't ! They want it for bad reasons ; not good ones like him.

CLARE. Do not forget charity, Brother !

JUNIPER. No, Sister. But it 's queer places one has to look round to find her, nowadays. They 've put her away. He wants her at his side to comfort him—so that he can smile and laugh, when the pain lets him. They won't let him smile : they won't let him laugh, either : it 's not holy enough for 'em.

CLARE. But he always has you, Brother.

JUNIPER. Yes, Sister ; but what can I do ? Playing the fool is all I 'm good for.

CLARE. That is where you are of such use to him, Juniper.

JUNIPER. Yes, Sister : but they don't think so. That 's why I was turned out and sent here—on ' an errand of charity.' . . . Do you know, Sister, I was tempted—sore tempted, I was—as soon as I 'd got through the gate where no one could see, to throw it all away and run back again, and just pretend I 'd brought it !

CLARE [*smiling*]. You did well, Brother, not to yield to the temptation.

[*A* Sister *appears within the grille as if to make request.* CLARE *beckons.*

Yes, Sisters, come and listen, all of you.

[*The* Sisters *appear, and stand looking out at* JUNIPER *through the grille.*

[*Then to* JUNIPER] For would not the little Father wish that we should have news of him ? Are not we also his sheep in another fold ? And is not his voice dear to us ?

JUNIPER. Yes, Sister.

CLARE. And who can bring him near to us better than you, Brother Juniper ? Had you come empty-handed you would have been as welcome.

[*Taking the basket from the hand of the* Lay-sister *she sets it outside again, while the* Lay-sister *goes on her errand to the garden.*

But had you not come at all you would have left us hungry and sorrowful, having no word of him. Did he send us no message ?

JUNIPER [*shaking his head*]. He was asleep, Sister. That's how they got me away—he being asleep, and knowing nothing of it.

CLARE. That is good news, Brother—that the little Father can sleep. Give me more news of him.

JUNIPER. Eh ! There he lies—just a bright shadow of himself—in the room the Bishop has lodged him. It's a great honour, so they tell me. Yes, I suppose ; but it isn't quiet and restful like Portiuncula would be. For all hours there's folk pushing in and out—peering at him ; and twice a day having him up to the window, showing him to

the people; and he too sick by rights to see anybody. 'Take me down to Portiuncula!' he says;
but his voice is all so weak now they pretend not
to hear him; so nothing's done. And he pining to
go, Sister! It's hard, hard treatment they're giving
him; but I can't make 'em do different—can I?

CLARE. Maybe no, Brother. So it is no fault
of yours.

JUNIPER. If it'd do him any good, me standing
on my head all day, or having myself beaten or
flayed alive for him—I wouldn't wish better than
to have it done to me.

CLARE. I well believe it, Brother.

JUNIPER. Yesterday—while 'twas going on—the
way I've been telling you—the little Father (he
can't see now, Sister; hardly at all with his eyes,
the light such a pain to 'em)—'Who's there?'
he says; and I say, 'It's me, Father; and there's
others waiting outside, wanting to have word of
you.' And so there were, Sister, and Father Elias
preaching to them—all about how holy he was,
there in the midst of us. Then the little Father
says to me—'Sing!' So I sang, Sister. And
you know what kind of a voice I've got. Then
he sang too; and a wonder it was where he got
his voice from—the Lord helping him; but like
enough, me being the stronger, there was more
noise than tune to it. So we'd hardly got started
when, killed of his preaching, in comes Father
Elias—eyes first—they were so out of his head,
Sister. 'You mustn't make that noise here!' he
says. 'We can't help it,' says the little Father,
'we are going to Heaven.' And then Father Elias,

58

to make a short bolt of it, tells him it's not the
proper and expected way for a saint to die in.
'Maybe not,' says the little Father; 'but it's
the right way for a sinner. For in all my sinful
life,' he says, 'I've never praised God as much
as I ought to do; so I'm making up for it now.'
Then Father Elias gets the Bishop to him—but
that's no good; for between them, the Bishop—
by God's mercy—hasn't a thought he can call his
own; so leaves it for the Doctor to say whether
or no it's good for him. And the Doctor, God
being merciful, says anything's good for him to do
now that pleases him, so long as it's within reason.
So then, Father Elias leaving us for a while, he
sends me for Brother Bernard, and Brother Giles,
and Brother John—not one of us with a voice you
can keep a tune to—that we may all sing joyfully
together—or separately maybe—according to how
we feel about it. So there we were, Sister, our
hearts full of the love of God and of the little Father
—making a great noise, like as he'd asked us
to—and Father Elias in and out the whole time,
on the flutter, like a cook when the pancakes are
burning—wanting it to stop, but not knowing how
—the Doctor having said it was good for him.
And when the little Father sleeps, we stop for a
while; and when he wakes we go on again. It's
a wonderful concert we've been having, Sister;
and a marvel how the little Father doesn't tire of
it. It's making a great scandal, Father Elias says,
and he fears if the Pope hears of it he'll not make
a saint of him. Is he doing it for a penance, do
you think, Sister?

CLARE. No, Brother.

JUNIPER. What for, then ?

CLARE. For love—of you, and the Brethren, and Portiuncula.

JUNIPER. Love ? I wish we all loved him as he loves us. Sister, what 's the use for us to say we love him, and then do all so different from what he 'd have us do ?

CLARE. That is what we are always doing to Christ, Brother, when we sin. And since we make Him suffer, must not the little Father suffer also, in like kind ?

JUNIPER. Yes, I suppose so. But it 's not fair to either ; is it, Sister ?

CLARE. No, Brother.

JUNIPER. Here, only the other day, we were bringing him back home again. 'Take me back to Assisi, soon,' he 'd told us. ' *Soon !* ' We knew what that meant : that if we were too long, he 'd never get there. So we were bringing him as fast as he could bear it—the shortest way, by Perugia. Then we heard, Sister, that in Perugia they wanted to catch him, and keep him—so that they might have his body !—and had sent out a band to lie in wait for him. Is that loving him ? Is that loving him, I say ?

CLARE. No, Brother : desire of possession is not love. But some day they will know better.

JUNIPER. Aye : ' possession.' And didn't the little Father say we were to have none ?

CLARE. Well, Brother ?

JUNIPER. So when Father Elias hears of it, he sends word we 're to go the other way, by Foligno.

And when they in Assisi hear of it—the citizens—
they send armed men to be a guard for him—
against them of Perugia. Oh, think of that
happening to *him*! Doesn't it hit your heart?
. . . When I saw them come out with swords and
with spears to take him, I thought of Him in the
garden at Gethsemane; and I wondered which
was going to kiss him for a sign to the rest. They
all kissed him, Sister—hands, feet, cord of his
girdle, hem of his robe! And the little Father
gave them a sweet blessing; but he was crying,
Sister. They were breaking his heart for him;
but he said nothing. 'Twasn't his life they cared
about, for the wonder that was in it: 'twas his
body, that's going to make them rich!

CLARE. But where his body lies, Brother, he
will not be.

JUNIPER. No, Sister.

CLARE. Therefore what they do to his body
matters little.

JUNIPER. No, Sister.

CLARE. Neither to him nor to any that truly love
him. Therefore, be of good cheer, Brother; as
he would have us be. And when you go back,
sing to him again, Brother.

JUNIPER. Ah! You comfort me, Sister. I knew
you could do it, if anybody.

CLARE. So now, Brother, return quickly: for
when he wakes again he will need you.

JUNIPER. I've a sort of fear, Sister, that
when I go back Father Elias is going to lock
me out.

CLARE. He will not, Brother. But if he did

there would still be others. Sister, have you brought what I told you ?

LAY-SISTER. They all have it, little Mother, between them. I gave it to them.

[*Through the grille one sees that each* Sister *has in her hand a few sprigs of lavender, which they have just received from the* Lay-sister.

CLARE. Here is some of our lavender, Brother. Give it to the little Father from all of us. Tell him it is from the bush which he planted : tell him it grows well, and is now full of flower. And when you give it him, give him our love, Brother ; and say that we all pray for him that he may have joy.

[*The* Sisters *stretch out their hands through the grille ;* JUNIPER *collects the lavender into one bunch. The* Sisters *surrender their gift with little murmurs of love.* JUNIPER *responds with nods and smiles. Meanwhile,* BROTHER JEROME *has entered, and is surveying the scene with an air not of entire approval. He waits, however, till the whole bunch is collected before speaking.*

JEROME. Brother Juniper, you are wanted.

JUNIPER [*turning in trepidation*]. Who wants me ?

JEROME. Father Minister, Brother Elias, wants you. . . . My Lord Bishop wants you. . . . And the little Father wants you.

JUNIPER. Holy Trinity ! All three of 'em. What 's happening now ?

JEROME. They are taking the little Father to Portiuncula. You are to go with him. The little Father will not start till you 're there to go with him.

THE ORDER OF RELEASE

[*With a whoop of joy, and a kick to the basket which lies in his way,* JUNIPER *makes a sprint across the stage and is off.*

JEROME [*calling after him*]. Brother Juniper— your basket!

CLARE. Aye! But run, run, Juniper! Oh, what a joyful pair of legs! The Lord be with them!

JEROME [*in tone of rebuke*]. The Lord does not rejoice in any man's legs, Sister.

CLARE. Perhaps not, Brother! But when a man's heart is in them, as Brother Juniper's is now —it becomes a question.

JEROME. Which I cannot discuss, Sister.

CLARE. No, Brother. O Sisters, how much ought we not to thank God for the making of this Juniper. There goes love to the little Father! Run, run, Juniper! Run!

[*Entirely oblivious to the disapproval of* BROTHER JEROME, *the* Sisters *all stand at the grille watching the departure of* JUNIPER; *and the excited motion of their hands through the grille is like the fluttering of doves in a cage.* JEROME *grudgingly picks up the basket left by* JUNIPER *and goes his disapproving way back to Assisi.*

CURTAIN

63

SISTER DEATH

Scene I. : Outside the cell of St. Francis.

Scene II. : Inside.

Both scenes have as their setting, or proscenium, a low broad archway extending almost the full breadth of the stage, with walls severely plain and unadorned, and side exits to right and left. Behind runs the breadth of a narrow corridor, to which the floor rises by two steps set in the thickness of the wall. Beyond that is the exterior of St. Francis' cell, occupying an angle of the corridor. Over the door of the cell, to left-centre, is a grille, and between the door and the corner of the passage a low niche or bench. Before the foreground arch two bell-ropes descend from the roof, and are hitched to the wall on each side.

In Scene II. everything beyond the corridor is removed to make way for the interior of St. Francis' cell, which thus appears on a raised level above the foreground.

Scene I. : On the bench sits BROTHER JUNIPER, *falling to sleep and jerking himself awake again. Enter* BROTHER RUFUS : *he unhitches the rope to the left, crosses himself and begins to ring for Angelus. Both before and while he does so, there has been knocking at the outer gate.*

RUFUS [*as he rings*]. Ave Maria, gratiae plena, Dominus tecum.

> [*The words go off into a mumble.* JUNIPER, *after trying mechanically to join in, desists : sleep overcoming him.*

Enter from the right, in haste, BROTHER HUMBLE, *with keys hanging from his girdle. At his back*

the knocking repeats itself.   Seeing BROTHER
RUFUS, *he halts.*

HUMBLE. Brother Rufus.

RUFUS [*raising his voice a little, to indicate that he is
doing a religious exercise, and is not to be interrupted*].
Sancta Maria, mater Dei, ora pro nobis peccatoribus
nunc et in hora mortis nostrae.

HUMBLE. Where 's Father Minister ?

RUFUS. Amen. . . . I know not, Brother.

HUMBLE. They 're at the gate again.   The Father
said I was to let in none.

RUFUS. Do as he tells you.   That 's what he told
me.

HUMBLE. They won't stop knocking.

RUFUS. Go, see who they are.

HUMBLE. I know already.   They came yesterday.
Now there 's more of them.

RUFUS. From Assisi ?

HUMBLE. Yes.   All the road 's black with them.

RUFUS [*hitching back the rope.*] They 're waiting for
the other bell to ring, to tell them that the Poverello 's dead !   Then they 'll feel safe, and sure of him.

HUMBLE [*going up to* JUNIPER, *and prodding him
softly*]. Brother Juniper. . . . Is Father Minister in
there ?

[JUNIPER *opens his eyes, looks at him without
intelligence, and shuts them again.*

RUFUS. Leave him !   He 's worn with watching.
Let him sleep !

HUMBLE. Then is the Poverello sleeping too ?

[*The knocking grows louder.*

RUFUS. If he were that would wake him.   Come,
come !   Get on !

HUMBLE. Oh, me ! The world, the world ! Eh ! How it 's with us !

[*He goes out ; the knocking gets more insistent.*

JUNIPER [*starting up*]. What for 's that knocking ?

RUFUS. Ears that will not hear, deafer than yours or mine. Nay, here he comes.

Enter the FATHER MINISTER, *preceded by* Brothers *carrying beams of wood and crowbars. They cross from left to right, taking their instructions by a backward glance, to which the* MINISTER *replies by a gesture.*

RUFUS. Father Minister, it 's the citizens again.

ELIAS. I know it, Brother.

RUFUS. There 's more of them now !

ELIAS. I know that also.

RUFUS. We shall need strong walls.

ELIAS. We have them. [*Loud knocking.*

RUFUS. And stronger gates.

ELIAS. Enough ! You need not fear.

RUFUS. There are more coming.

ELIAS. All the world may come ! They shall not spoil us of him.

[*A fresh thunder of knocking.* JUNIPER, *who has risen at the entry of* ELIAS, *and has watched with apprehension the carrying of the beams, now stumbles forward and kneels at the side of his Superior.*

JUNIPER. O Father Minister ! Don't keep them from him : let him die in peace !

ELIAS. Go back to your post, Brother.

RUFUS. Father, last night I was at the gate. She that you spoke of came—the Lady Giacomina.

ELIAS. At what hour ?

RUFUS. 'Twas midnight, Father.

ELIAS. Yes ?

RUFUS. I sent her away.

Enter BROTHER HUMBLE *hurriedly. Seeing the* FATHER MINISTER, *he stops, makes obeisance, and waits permission to speak.*

ELIAS. My son, what is it ?

HUMBLE. The citizens demand speech with you, Father.

ELIAS. They ' demand,' do they ?

HUMBLE. Aye. There 's a great crowd. It 's growing, Father.

ELIAS. Take others with you. Bid the crowd stand back ; then let in three.

[Exit BROTHER HUMBLE.

RUFUS. I think we shall need help.

ELIAS. Help is at hand. In the Sacristy we have arms.

JUNIPER [*kneeling at the door of the cell*]. O little lover of men, pray for us sinners now in the hour of thy death !

ELIAS. She came last night, you say ?

RUFUS. With her two sons : In great haste, Father, having journeyed far.

ELIAS. Wherefor ?

RUFUS. Wishing to see him ere he died.

ELIAS. How did she know ? You did not send his letter ?

RUFUS. No, Father, no ! She said that she had heard the Poverello calling to her : ' Sister ! Sister Giacomina ! '—his very voice, Father !

ELIAS. And you ?

RUFUS. I said that he was very near his end ; and could see nobody. 'Earthly things,' I said, ' he hath put away—all frailties, all affections, all desires,—giving himself to God.' As you told me, so I told her, Father.

ELIAS. What said she then ?

RUFUS. She wept. Oh ! very grievously she wept, begging to be let in. There, at the gate, I left her— weeping.

ELIAS. Thus, at the last, disguised in charity, the Devil comes tempting him,—seeking, by subtle ways of mortal weakness, to dim his glory.

Enter HUMBLE, *followed by three* Citizens, *and several* Friars : *from the opposite side other* Friars *enter.*

HUMBLE. Here they are, Father Minister.

ELIAS. Why have ye come ?

1ST CITIZEN. Shortly—to speak with you.

ELIAS. I heard that you had orders for me. No ?

1ST CITIZEN. Only to make request.

ELIAS. Well, let us hear it ?

1ST CITIZEN. The Poverello, Father ; lives he still ?

ELIAS. He lives ; he hath slept ; he is awake again. [*The* Citizens *exchange looks.*

1ST CITIZEN. That is good news, Father Minister ; very good news. We come to see him.

ELIAS. Ye may not.

2ND CITIZEN. Out yonder they expect it.

ELIAS. I am sorry. Be patient awhile.

3RD CITIZEN. Patient ! Till when ?

ELIAS. [*making the sign of the Cross*]. Till he be dead. If ye beheld him now ye would not know him.

2ND CITIZEN. But we should know the marks,— the miracle, Father.

3RD CITIZEN. Aye! Let us see those!

ELIAS. Adulterous generation! Ye seek a sign. But it shall not be given.

1ST CITIZEN. We seek naught but our own. His body belongs——

ELIAS. To God, Brother.

2ND CITIZEN. To Assisi.

3RD CITIZEN. Here was he born, and here shall he be buried!

1ST CITIZEN. Here in San Giorgio. The city demands it.

ELIAS. What is your fear?

2ND CITIZEN. A body gone to Rome!

1ST CITIZEN. Look: when he dies, he will become a saint: work miracles, and all the world will hear, and flock like crows. So, where the body lies, the glory of him will be.

3RD CITIZEN. And all the fame.

2ND CITIZEN. So give us surety—first that he bides here now; next that ye take him not, when he is dead, wholly away from us.

3RD CITIZEN. Nay, nor in pieces either! Ye would do that which in the wilderness was done with bread; and by your miracles so multiply him, till all our honour and profit of him be gone.

1ST CITIZEN. The body is ours, Father; and we be here to see to it!

ELIAS. Living or dead, he is in God's hands, Brother.

1ST CITIZEN. Aye, when we have the holding up of them ! But now he is in yours, and in the hands of my Lord Bishop : and that means of Rome.

2ND CITIZEN. Thither he goes not !
　　　　　　[Murmurs are heard from the crowd.

1ST CITIZEN. Hark ! Yonder be men, hungry for what is theirs, and *shall* be theirs : else, from this place we stir not.

2ND CITIZEN. Nor shall any !

3RD CITIZEN. Whole or in pieces ; be he alive or dead—he goes not hence ! If here we find him not, we 'll tear your roof down.

ELIAS. Enough ! I 'll hear no more. Hence, get you gone ! 　　*[The murmurs of the crowd increase.*

1ST CITIZEN. Nothing comes out till we have seen the body.

ELIAS. Go : for ye shall not !

2ND CITIZEN. Take not too long over his dying, Father Minister ! The people grow impatient.

ELIAS. Forth with these brawlers ! Go ! Bar up the gates !
　　[The Friars *take hold of the three* Citizens *and begin thrusting them out.*

1ST CITIZEN. We are not gone, Father !

2ND CITIZEN. We 'll see you starve !

3RD CITIZEN. Bark ! Bite !—Skin the whole pack of you ! 　　*[They go out, forced by the* Brethren.

RUFUS. Of a truth, Father,—doth he yet live ?

ELIAS. Aye, so,—by a great miracle. Come, Brothers, to the Sacristy ; arm yourselves !
　　*[*JUNIPER *runs forward and kneels before the* FATHER MINISTER.

JUNIPER. O Father Minister, let them come in !

Let them come in, Father ! They have but to look
on his face, they will be blest ! Let them see him,
and they will be satisfied.

> [*The* FATHER MINISTER *goes out, followed by*
> *others.*

LEO. Come, Brother. We must obey.

JUNIPER. No, no ! They are killing him ! If he
hears tell of it, he 'll die ! Oh, don't die, Father
dear ! Don't die ! Don't die !

> [*Exit* LEO, JUNIPER *kneels at the cell door.*

O Lord, be merciful to him ! O Lord, give him
peace ! Give him peace !

> [*A clattering of arms is heard.* JUNIPER *stops*
> *his ears, and bows weeping at the door of the cell.*

CURTAIN

SISTER DEATH

Scene II.: Inside the cell. FRANCIS *lies stretched on a trestle bed,* JUNIPER *sits at the foot watching him. Across the window a curtain is drawn. One whole side of the cell lies open toward the corridor which runs between it and the arch.*

FRANCIS. Brother Juniper.

JUNIPER. Aye, Father ?

FRANCIS. Where is . . . Brother Light ?

JUNIPER [*lifting a corner of the curtain*]. He 's here, Father,—looking at you.

FRANCIS. Draw—draw it, Brother ! [JUNIPER *draws back the curtain.*] Welcome, Light ! Oh, welcome, Light !

JUNIPER. Have you slept, Father ?

FRANCIS. In my life more times than I ought, Brother. So now I must pay back what I owe.

JUNIPER. Then you did not sleep, Father ?

FRANCIS. Sister Sleep came and looked at me, but could not stay.

JUNIPER. Are you in pain, Father ?

FRANCIS. All night long she was my comforter. She is here still.

JUNIPER. What will I do for you, Father ?

FRANCIS. Sing to me, Juniper.

JUNIPER. Mine is an ugly voice, Father.

FRANCIS. So is Brother Frog's; yet doth he praise God for it.

JUNIPER. Shall I praise God for my ugly voice?

FRANCIS. Often have I praised Him for it: it hath been very sweet to me.

JUNIPER. Our mouths are foul things, Father.

FRANCIS. So are our bodies; yet we thank God for them, and for our other afflictions also.

JUNIPER. Aye, so we do, Father. 'Tis a great mystery.

FRANCIS. Therefore, sing, Brother.

JUNIPER. What shall I sing?

FRANCIS. Of light, Brother, and water, and fire, and Mother Earth. Hast thou forgot what I taught thee?

JUNIPER [*making the sign of the Cross*]. In nomine Patris, et Filii, et Spiritus Sancti.

> Praised be my Lord for all being,
> And namely praise for our Brother Sun,
> Who bringeth us day and light for seeing;
> With joy he cometh his course to run.

FRANCIS [*feebly, in a whisper, with pauses*].

> Praised be my Lord for Brother Wind,
> And air, and cloud, and calms of weather;
> Whereby all creatures Thou dost bind
> Into one fellowship together.

JUNIPER.

> Praised be my Lord for Brother Fire,
> By whom comes light through the darkness long;
> Warm, and pleasant, and dear to desire,
> Mighty is he and very strong.

FRANCIS.

> Praised be my Lord for Sister Water;
> Ever of service hath she been,

Waiting on men, sweet running Water,
She is humble, and precious, and clean.

[*While he sings the rest of the* Brothers *enter
very quietly, and move gradually nearer.
They have concealed under their habits long
daggers, maces and swords.*

JUNIPER. Praised be my Lord, for all who give
Pardon to others for His love's sake,

FRANCIS. And meekly endure in pains to live;
In Him they rest, and in Him shall wake.

JUNIPER. Praised be my Lord for Sister Death . . .
No mortal body shall she spare. . . .

[*He begins weeping.*

FRANCIS. Brother Frog, why hast thou ceased
singing?

JUNIPER. I cannot more, Father.

FRANCIS. Who is here?

LEO. All of us, Father.

FRANCIS. All? Wherefor? Is it a feast?

LEO. Not a feast, a vigil, Father.

JUNIPER [*weeping*]. O Father, for the love of
God, don't, don't go and leave us!

FRANCIS. We are all in God, Brother.

JUNIPER. Ah, you may talk, you may talk,
Father! And I'm a sinner, and we be all sinners;
—and the Lord isn't in us—not yet: only now and
again, maybe, when we aren't thinking of Him.

FRANCIS. Where is Father Minister?

RUFUS. He is not here, little Father.

LEO. He has been called away. You wish to see
him, Father?

FRANCIS. Aye!

LEO. I will tell him.   [*Exit* LEO.

75

FRANCIS. Juniper.

JUNIPER. Yes, Father?

FRANCIS. Where is Sister Giacomina?

JUNIPER. Surely, I know not.

FRANCIS. Did she not come?

JUNIPER. No, Father.

FRANCIS. Last night—who came?

JUNIPER. None that I know of, Father.

FRANCIS. There was a bell, and knocking at the gate; and voices—I thought I knew.

JUNIPER. Ah! Why must you choose to lie so nearby, Father: and hear all the ringing and the knocking?

FRANCIS. Sister Bell hath a sweet sound.

JUNIPER. Aye; to them that like hearing her.

FRANCIS. Sister Giacomina . . . why tarriest thou?

[RUFUS *stands conscience-stricken: other* Brothers
kneel to pray. *Enter* GILES, *bringing food.*

Father Minister hath not come?

BERNARD. No, Father.

GILES. Here is food for you, little Father.

FRANCIS. Not yet, little Brother. . . . Other sheep I have, not of this fold; them also must I bring.

GILES. Nay, but for our sake, Father, so that we may have joy in thee. Eat, I pray thee, of thy son's venison.

FRANCIS. Bleat not, little sheep! . . . When I eat . . . ye shall all eat with me. . . . Brother Rufus.

RUFUS. Father?

FRANCIS. When thou art at the gate, I bid thee think always of sweet Sister Charity. . . . Brothers, why are ye so silent?

BERNARD. We were praying, Father.

FRANCIS. I pray that your prayers be all answered.

[RUFUS *utters a sharp sob, stumbles forward, and kneels down before* FRANCIS.

RUFUS. Father . . . I was at the gate last night but had not charity.

FRANCIS. Wast thou so, Brother ?

RUFUS. Ah, pardon me that I did not bring thee good !

FRANCIS. Good is with God, Brother.

RUFUS. Ah, pardon that I failed not to do thee harm !

FRANCIS. What harm, Brother ?

RUFUS. I sent her away, Father ! She came, and I sent her away !

FRANCIS. Who ?

RUFUS. Sweet Sister Charity, and the Lady Giacomina.

FRANCIS. Sister Giacomina ! . . . Now I know thy mind was to be with me. . . . Brother, I thank thee for thy news. Thou hast given me—joy. . . . How seemed she ?

Re-enter BROTHER LEO.

RUFUS. Very eager, Father, very sorrowful, and tender to any word of thee. Two young men, her sons, stood by her. I left them weeping.

FRANCIS. Welcome, Sister Tears ! . . . Brothers, leave me alone awhile. Do not go far ! Juniper, stay near me.

[*They retire to the forecourt.* JUNIPER *stays between.*

JUNIPER. You will take care of yourself, Father ?

FRANCIS. Sister Care will be with me.

JUNIPER. Make thy peace with her, Father ; for often thou hast neglected her.

FRANCIS. So I will, Brother.

> [*Kneeling in the forecourt, the* Brothers *begin praying. Now and then between the words of* FRANCIS, *the deep mutter of their praying is heard, beginning loud and dying away.*

BROTHERS. Domine, Domine, Deus salutis meae, in die clamavi, et nocte coram te : intret oratio mea in conspectu tuo, Domine ! Ostende mihi, Domine, misericordiam tuam !

FRANCIS. Sister Care, come and let me see thy face ! Why art thou so worn, and sorrowful ! Surely thou hast wept long, and hast neither eaten nor slept. Go to sleep, Sister Care ! I will watch over thee.

Enter FATHER MINISTER. *He stands behind for a while ;* JUNIPER, *by signals, informs him that* FRANCIS *has asked to be left alone. He kneels, facing away from* FRANCIS *toward the kneeling Brotherhood.*

BROTHERS. Redime me, Domine, et miserere mei. Exaudi, Deus, orationem meam, et ne despexeris deprecationem meam ; intende in me, et exaudi me. Aufer a me iniquitates meas.

FRANCIS. Ay, come, be not afraid ! Hide not thyself from me now ! Come, Sister Pain, let me look on thee, let me taste thy breath. Ah, thou art heavy, thou art heavy upon me, Sister Pain. Pity thy poor ass that stumbles because of his load ! Lo,

to left, lo, to right, where shall I turn me now ?　O
Angel of the Lord, which standest before me in the
way,—O flaming sword, why keepest thou me from
Paradise ?　Have I not loved thee enough, Sister
Pain ?　Have I not learned all things from thee,
whose eyes did look into the eyes of my dying Lord,
—yea, the lips, yea, the eyes, yea, the sweet breast !
O Christ, Thou lover of men, Thou lover of men !

ELIAS. Now cometh he to the Cross. Now is he
with Christ !

BROTHERS. Corpus Domini nostri, Jesu Christi,
custodiat animam meam in vitam aeternam.

FRANCIS. Yea, this is a field, and these be flowers
that I see ! Pluck not these, Brother, which have
but one limb to hold up heads to the light. Give
them thy hand, Brother, give them thy hand !

ELIAS. Now he doth look upon Paradise.

BROTHERS. Ecce Agnus Dei, ecce qui tollit peccata
mundi.

FRANCIS. Brother Juniper !
　　　　　　　　　[*He tries to lift himself but fails.*

JUNIPER. Father ?

FRANCIS. Thou art simple, Brother Juniper, but
thou art wise.

JUNIPER. I was never wise, Father ; God forbid !

FRANCIS. Thou didst speak truth to me, when I
would not hear.

JUNIPER. Did I so, Father ?

FRANCIS. For now is my body past use, and yet I
live. . . . Brother Ass, I have been too hard on
thee !

JUNIPER [*weeping*]. I told thee of it, Father.
Often I told thee !

79

FRANCIS. Bear me—bear me out into the light!
> [*Two* Brothers *carry his bed out into the space before the cell, while the rest continue to pray audibly.* JUNIPER *kneels weeping at his side.*

FRANCIS. Father Minister. . . . [ELIAS *comes and stands near him.*] I pray you lift my hand and lay it on the head of this Juniper. [ELIAS *does so.*] The Lord hath set His mark on thee. [JUNIPER *retires.*] . . . Brother Leo. . . . [LEO *comes forward and kneels;* ELIAS *assists the hand of* FRANCIS.] . . . The Lord bless and keep thee! The Lord make His face to shine on thee! . . . [LEO *retires.*] . . . Brother Bernard. [*The same action is repeated.*] . . . Brother Giles, bleat not, little sheep. . . . Brother Conrad. . . . Brother Masseo, the Lord strengthen thee! . . . Brother Rufus, the Lord open to thee! . . . Brother Simon . . . Brother Angelo . . . Brother Jerome, the Lord be a light unto thee! . . . Brother John. . . . Father Minister Elias, I thank thee!

ELIAS [*kneeling*]. Bless me also, O my Father!

FRANCIS [*taking the cord of* ELIAS's *girdle, and kissing it*]. The Lord hath given thee my flock: be thou its blessing! . . .
> [*The* FATHER MINISTER *rises, and signals to two of the* Brothers. *They go out, and presently return: one lights the death-candles, the other bears a Cross.*

FRANCIS. Ah, now cometh Sister Joy! Take thou my hand and lead me, so that I may see light! [*The sun shines full on him.*] See, oh, see! He cometh, He cometh!

O Brother Sun,
Rejoicing thou dost run
Unto all lands !
Therefore, I bid thee take
This heart in thy hands,
Of a poor little one
Whose journeyings are all done.

BROTHERS. Miserere mei, Deus, secundum magnam misericordiam tuam, etc.   (Psalm 51.)

FRANCIS. And when thou dost make
To rise from thy wings
A new East, and dost wake
(For our dear Lord's sake)
Where new day begins—
Beast, reptile, and bird,
Cattle, and herd,
And all creeping things ;
Then cry for me
Unto all thou dost see,
' On a Tree of great mercy
Christ died for thee ! '

[*The* Cross-bearer *takes his stand at the foot of
the bed.*

BROTHERS. Domine, clamavi ad te : exaudi me :
intende voci meae, cum clamavero ad te, etc.
(Psalm 140.)

FRANCIS. O Brother Sun,
How swiftly thou goest
The way thou knowest,
Now my day is done !
Bear me in the beams
Of thy light as it streams

From East unto West,
Till I come to the breast
Of the Life I love best!
There shall I find rest.

BROTHERS. De profundis clamavi ad te, Domine:
Domine, exaudi vocem meam. Si iniquitates observaveris, Domine, Domine, quis sustinebit?

[*The* Friars *cease praying. Outside is heard a
murmuring of the crowd.*

FRANCIS. Now see I the body of Christ multi-
plied for men! Not as bread, nor on the altar doth
it show: but in the homes, and the highways
and the market-places, manifest through flesh and
blood. . . . This is His Body which was given
for me.

BERNARD. Look! He hath a vision!

FRANCIS. Bread! Give me bread, Brother!

[GILES *brings bread.* FRANCIS *takes, and breaks
it as he is speaking.*

O Lord, Lover Christ, when saw I Thee hungry, or
sick, or poor, or in prison, and have not ministered
unto Thee?

[*A breath of wonder escapes the listening* Friars.

ELIAS. Peace! [*The murmurs of the crowd grow
louder.*

FRANCIS. This I break . . .
This take . . .
For Love's sake!

[*He gives the bread to* FATHER ELIAS, *who gives
part of it to* BROTHER BERNARD; *and together they distribute it to the kneeling*
Brothers.

FRANCIS. Take. . . . Take. . . . Take. . . .

Enter BROTHER HUMBLE, *running.*

HUMBLE. Father Minister, Father Minister ! . . . They are crying for him, Father, they are tearing at the gates !

ELIAS. Go ! Quickly—some of you !

FRANCIS. Take. . . . Take. . . . Take. . . .

> [*Several of the* Brothers *accompany* HUMBLE *to the gate. Cries are heard :* ' Bring out the Poverello ! Bring out the Poverello ! ' *The shoutings and confusion increase.*

JUNIPER. O Father, he's dying; he's dying, Father ! Don't fight for him ! Let him die in peace !

FRANCIS. Take. . . . Take. . . .

ELIAS. Toll the bell, Brother !

> [JUNIPER, *weeping and beating his breast, runs to the bell and begins tolling it. As he does so the noise of clamour ceases ; a moan of love and tenderness rises from the crowd and dies away.*

FRANCIS. Take. . . . Take. . . . Take. . . .

> [*He falls back exhausted as he comes to the last.*

O Bread of Life ! O Body of Love ! O Maker of men !

> [*The tolling of the bell goes on. The voice of the crowd is heard, chanting the* ' De Profundis.'

FRANCIS. Open ! Open the gates of Righteousness !

RUFUS. He bids me open the gate, Father ! On holy obedience, Father, *let* me open the gate ! Father, I *must* open the gate !

THE BROTHERS. He must, Father, he must open the gate !

> [*Faced by this spiritual revolt within the community, the* FATHER MINISTER *yields.*

[JUNIPER *stops tolling, and stands rapt, expectant.
The rest kneel. The* Cross-bearer *lifts the Cross
high.*

FRANCIS. Take ! . . . I thank. . . . I thank. . . .

ELIAS [*kneeling at the feet of* FRANCIS]. Give us
thy blessing, Father, for we are sinners !

FRANCIS. O Word made Flesh ! O Body of Love !
O Maker of men ! Take ! . . .

[*He tries to speak further, but fails.*

ELIAS. Yea, tell us, Father !

FRANCIS. Man is His making, Brother ! Man is
His making !

ELIAS. Aye : till by man came sin.

FRANCIS. Without . . . man . . . Christ . . . were
not . . . made. . . . Without . . . man . . . Christ . . .
were not . . . made. Without . . . man . . . [*The
death struggle begins.*]

Re-enter Brothers, *followed by the crowd, singing
the ' De Profundis.' All bare their heads and
kneel.* ELIAS *rises.*

ELIAS [*making the sign of the Cross*]. Requiem
aeternam dona ei, Domine, et lux perpetua luceat ei.

[*All cross themselves and wait in silence. The
sun sinks, and the stage darkens.*

FRANCIS. Welcome, Sister Death !

[*He stretches out his arms.* BROTHERS LEO *and*
BERNARD *support them. He stays motionless
for a while. It grows darker. He rises in
their arms with a last effort.*

Welcome, Brother Sun !   [*He falls back dead.*

CURTAIN

SISTER DEATH

Before the Curtain comes the Cross-bearer, *and speaks.*

O Brother Sun,
Rejoicing, thou dost run
Unto all lands !
Therefore, I bid thee take
This heart in thy hands,
Of a poor little one
Whose journeyings are all done :
And when thou dost make
To rise from thy wings
A new East, and dost wake
(For our dear Lord's sake)
Where new day begins,—
Beast, reptile, and bird,
Cattle and herd,
And all creeping things ;
Then cry for me
Unto all thou dost see,—
' On a Tree of great mercy
Christ died for thee.'

GATE OF LIFE

Across the background runs a high wall. In the centre a broad gateway, closed in by a grille, through which comes a broken view of hillside and sky. To right and left stand the conventual buildings of St. Damiens, narrow windows and doors with steps leading up to them.

A group of the Poor Clare Sisters stand pressed to the gate: another Sister, with hands clasped, is gazing from the steps to the right, over their heads, in tense expectation. Hurriedly from without comes a Lay Sister; they draw back to make way for her, she opens the gate and comes through.

LAY SISTER. Oh! They are coming, Sisters!

[She closes the gate.

1ST SISTER. Go quickly! Tell Reverend Mother!

2ND SISTER [on steps]. She knows, Sister.

[Hardly has she said this when, with a catch of the breath, she turns to find CLARE standing behind her. She draws aside, CLARE enters, and goes to the gate. The Sisters make way for her, and stand back, a little in awe at a grief which they feel to be greater than their own. On this day, for the first time, their love for their Reverend Mother is mixed with fear. She stands looking out in rigid composure, only the clenched lips and hands indicate strong emotion.

1ST SISTER. They are coming, Mother dear. Sister Angela has seen them.

[CLARE *makes no sign of hearing her.*

LAY SISTER. Yes, Reverend Mother, a great crowd. The whole city has come out to follow him. Down there the road is full of them.

3RD SISTER. If they go by the road, we shan't see him !

[*This causes cries of lamentation among the* Sisters.

1ST SISTER. But we SHALL see him, shan't we, Mother ? They won't go by without letting us see him, will they, Mother ?

CLARE [*after a pause*]. No, Sister.

2ND SISTER. Father Minister Elias promised : didn't he, Mother dear ?

[*A pause. There is no answer. They have now crowded to the gate again.*

3RD SISTER. Oh, look, they are still going along the road. The *crowd* isn't coming ! The *crowd* isn't coming, Mother !

CLARE. He is coming, Sister.

4TH SISTER [*pushing forward*]. Let me ! I can't see anything !

5TH SISTER. Yes ! Yes ! But I can ! There ! There ! They *are* coming ! They are coming !

3RD SISTER. Yes, it 's *he*. They are bringing him !

[*Her voice breaks saying it.* CLARE *turns away from gate.*

1ST SISTER [*catching sight of* CLARE'S *face, kneels and kisses her sleeve*]. Mother ! Little Mother !

2ND SISTER. S-sh !

[*Awe is upon them. Silently they draw back.*

CLARE is left standing alone. Distant chanting is heard. The words of the ' De Profundis ' are being sung. The Sisters stand motionless; the singing draws nearer. As it approaches, CLARE kneels; the Sisters kneel with her.

CLARE. Almighty God, with Whom do live the spirits of just men made perfect, and in Whom the souls of all that die faithfully find joy and felicity, we give Thee thanks that it hath pleased Thee to take this our Brother and Father out of the bondage of the flesh into the freedom of the Life eternal. We praise Thee, we bless Thee, we glorify Thee for the joy wherein now he dwells ; and may we, with him, be found worthy in the Body of Thy Christ, at His second coming, there to be all made one.

[*The chanting grows louder, drowning the voice of CLARE, who continues to pray aloud, the Sisters all responding.*

CLARE. Lord, have mercy upon us !

SISTERS. Christ, have mercy upon us !

CLARE. Lord, have mercy upon us !

[*The head of the procession is now passing the gate. First come Friars, then incense-bearers, then a Priest; then a cross borne high, so that it is seen advancing above the wall. Then follows an open bier, on the shoulders of four Friars, bearing the body of FRANCIS. The procession halts.*

SISTERS. Little Father ! Little Father !

CLARE. Nearer, Brothers ; come nearer ! [*They do so, bringing the bier close to the grille.*] Lower. [*They kneel, still supporting the bier ; ELIAS appears on the further side of it.*]

CLARE. Father Minister. . . . Your blessing, Father.

> [*With a murmured 'Dominus Vobiscum,'* ELIAS *makes toward them the sign of the Cross.*

Father Minister, of your charity, give us the hand of our little Father, now dead, that he also may bless us !

> [*The hand of* FRANCIS *is lifted and passed through the grille.* CLARE *with extended hand supporting it, all the* Sisters *come weeping, and kiss it in turn. Meanwhile,* CLARE *is speaking.*

From this hand came deeds of love. From this hand came blessing. From this hand came showing of wisdom, and guidance for us all. From this hand we received, into our own lives, of the Body of Christ—that in Him we may all become one.

> [CLARE *alone does not kiss the hand. With the fingers of her disengaged hand she touches the dead flesh, then raises her own hand to her lips, kisses, and signs herself with the Cross.*

Requiem eternam ei, Domine ; et lux perpetua luceat ei. Amen.

> [*Sounds of weeping from the* Sisters. *The hand is withdrawn ; the bier is raised again.*

Farewell, little Father ! We shall meet again.

> [*Voices begin the ' Nunc Dimittis.' The procession goes on its way. All the* Sisters, *except* CLARE, *are weeping. They kneel watching as the body is borne away.* CLARE *is the first to rise. She touches the shoulder of the* LAY SISTER, *and directs her with a slight gesture.*

The LAY SISTER *goes quickly. Almost at once a bell is heard—swift not loud—ringing the Community to prayer. They rise obediently and pass into the Chapel. The bell stops. The* LAY SISTER *returns.* CLARE, *who has not looked out again, is about to follow, when a figure comes stumbling to the grille, staggers, catches hold, and leans against it.* CLARE *has already reached the door, when she hears and turns.*

CLARE [*as she goes toward him*]. Brother Juniper !

JUNIPER. Aye : what 's left of him !

CLARE. Come in, Brother.

JUNIPER. Oh, don't speak to me ! Don't look at me ! I 'm deaf and blind ! Deaf and blind, Sister ! Deaf and blind !

CLARE. Open, Sister ! Nay, but you are in the way, Brother.

[*She touches him, he moves aside ; the* LAY SISTER *opens the wicket.*

Come in, Brother !

JUNIPER. Am I to come in, Sister ?

CLARE. Why, surely ! Who could be more welcome to us—now ?

JUNIPER. Aye ! ' *Now, now !* ' Isn't it like a bell tolling ? ' *Now !* '

CLARE. Some day this ' now ' will be very sweet to us. Yes, go, Sister !

[*The* LAY SISTER *goes to join the others.*

JUNIPER. Not for me, Sister, never ! I 'm finished. Done for ! Dark 's the sun ; and its touch on me like a dead hand.

CLARE. But there are living hands still, Brother.

JUNIPER. They don't need me ! They don't want me ; nor I—I don't want them.

CLARE. More now than ever, Brother.

JUNIPER. Eh ? For why, then ?

CLARE. For better remembrance—of *him*.

JUNIPER. Remembrance ? [*He unslings a pair of sandals.*] Aye ! That 's all that 's left to me now. Look ! I 've brought you these. They were the little Father's ; the last he ever wore. The last time his feet went walking was in these. Now they 're for you, Sister.

CLARE. For remembrance. God reward you for your charity, Brother.

JUNIPER. Eh, but they 're not mine, Sister. They were *his* ; so they belong to nobody. The first time we ever met—' Oh, master,' I said, ' will it give you joy if I make a pair of shoes for you ? ' He said I might, so I did. He wore 'em. But I didn't make *these* for him ; he didn't let me. They were just some that he 'd picked up anywhere—given to him, or maybe just thrown away. But now—just for his feet having been in them—they 're worth more than anything you could name !

CLARE. So likewise is the worth of the world, Brother.

JUNIPER. Why the world ?

CLARE. He having been in it.

JUNIPER. But gone.

CLARE. *God* is still in it, Brother ; and Sister World still needs us.

JUNIPER. Aye, that 's the trouble ! How am I to love it, and care for it, still ? I can't, Sister !

CLARE. Not to-day, Brother ; but to-morrow.

JUNIPER. No, Sister. To-day's dark. To-morrow's shadow of it will be darker.

CLARE. But this very day, Brother, you had thought and care for us; and to-morrow you will care for us still, as much as ever.

JUNIPER. For you? Aye. *You* all loved him.

CLARE. Some day all the world will love him! And your love for the world will then have helped.

JUNIPER. How can I help all the world—a fool like me?

CLARE. Even as you helped *him*, Brother—by your foolishness. For in your foolishness you often do and say wise things without knowing it.

JUNIPER. How? When?

CLARE. *You* brought us these shoes, Brother. Who else would have thought of it?

JUNIPER. Being a shoemaker: that's all.

CLARE. A good reason, Brother, if it brings good to us. So with everything. Why are you here now, Brother?

JUNIPER. I came from where I wasn't wanted, Sister: that's all.

CLARE. That also was a good reason, Brother. Yet those who want you least now, will some day want more of you.

JUNIPER. Father Elias will never want me.

CLARE. There was a time when you did not want the little Father.

JUNIPER. Before I'd seen him, that was. I'm wanting him now; but what's the use, when all's over?

CLARE. 'All' is never over, Brother. All has only begun—and we but a small part of it.

JUNIPER. Not for me, Sister.

CLARE. Why not ?

JUNIPER. Finished—done !

CLARE. Have you finished and done loving him, Brother ?

JUNIPER. No, no, Sister dear ! God forbid !

CLARE. He left his love to the world, in weak vessels—you and me. But while we hold together —'tis *in* us.

JUNIPER [*searching deep*]. What *is* love, Sister ?

CLARE. Love is God, Brother.

JUNIPER [*scared*]. Have we got God in *us* ?

CLARE. We are *in* God, Brother.

JUNIPER [*feeling his way*]. In love, eh ? But blind to it.

CLARE. In so far as we love, we are *in* God, and our little Father in God with us.

JUNIPER. He was *all* love, wasn't he ?

CLARE. To us he seemed so.

JUNIPER. Yet he always doubted himself.

CLARE. But not God, Brother.

JUNIPER. But how can that be, Sister ?—to be like love himself, yet to doubt it ?

CLARE [*pointing*]. See, Brother ; there is a cloud full of light—yet to the earth it casts a shadow. For though it be filled with light, it cannot give out such light as that which comes to it. Looking earthward the cloud sees only its own shadow ; but looking heavenward, sees light. So earthward from us goes doubt, while out of Heaven comes knowledge.

JUNIPER [*groping for light*]. The little Father ! In *his* shadow there was light.

CLARE. Shadows being from God, Brother.

JUNIPER. *His* shadow.

CLARE. So this shadow of his dying is from God also.

JUNIPER. Pray for me, Sister, for I am blind !

CLARE. Thy blindness, Brother, is also a shadow, and is from God ; and, when God so wills it, will pass from thee.

[JUNIPER *looks at her wistfully. There is silence between them for a while. Comes the distant tolling of a bell.* JUNIPER *starts and shivers.*

JUNIPER. Hark ! They are tolling for him !

CLARE. No matter. He hears it not.

JUNIPER. But we do ! We do ! [*The tolling continues.*] And if that were to stop, in my heart it would go on.

CLARE. Go, then, Brother ! If it be in thy heart, follow the sound !

JUNIPER. No need : it comes to me here, Sister.

[*The tolling goes on. They listen, till again* CLARE *speaks.*

CLARE. The little Father lives still, Brother. Further than that bell goes his sound. Men will know of him.

JUNIPER. Yes, Sister ; but they won't see or hear him any more—not to know as *we* know.

CLARE. God does not depend on man's senses, Brother.

JUNIPER. No : else where would I be ?

CLARE. Often He uses means we could not, and with them works wonder. You, with but little sense, Brother, have more faith than many of us : with less learning, more love : with less understanding, more wisdom.

JUNIPER. Maybe—so long as *he* taught me.

CLARE. He does still, Brother.

JUNIPER. Aye, but it 's to sorrow now.

CLARE. Sorrow well, Brother ; but rejoice also.

JUNIPER. Hark ! There 's more tolling. Now they are burying him.

[*A* MENDICANT *appears at gate, and touches it with groping hands.*

CLARE. Only his body. We still see the sun he saw—the world he loved. And why he loved it, we know ; and for the same reason must love it also.

JUNIPER. Not as he did, Sister. He 'd a heart for everything. We can't be like him.

CLARE. All likes are not equal, Brother ; but the stream runs to the river, and the river to the sea !

[*While they have been speaking the old* MENDI-CANT *stands waiting patiently at the gate. Curiously motionless and without life he stands waiting.*

JUNIPER. Look ! Who 's there at the gate, Sister ?

CLARE. Ah ! Was he waiting ? Go, Brother ! He 's blind ; open and bring him in !

[JUNIPER *goes, opens, and brings him in.*

JUNIPER. The little Sister says you are to come in.

CLARE. He doesn't hear you, Brother.

JUNIPER. How d'you know that ?

CLARE. Because he has been here before.

MENDICANT [*feeling doubtfully at the hand which is touching him*]. Who—who is it ? [*His voice is even and toneless, as though his tongue also were feeling its way.*]

JUNIPER. Ye 're deaf ; so I 'm nobody.

MENDICANT. I don't know you. What are you doing with me?

JUNIPER. What am I doing with him, Sister?

CLARE. Bring him here, Brother; here. Let him sit down.

JUNIPER [*as he does so*]. There! That's what I'm doing with you. Don't stiffen yourself! There's a seat for you.

[*The* MENDICANT *sits down;* CLARE *goes and touches him. The* MENDICANT *feels hand, arm, and robe.*

MENDICANT. Ah! It's the dear Lady! Sure, sure, sure! Come and sit where I can be sure of you.

[CLARE *sits down beside him.* JUNIPER *is looking on, much amazed.*

JUNIPER. Now how's that, Sister? Can't see; can't hear. But knows you, and can talk! How?

CLARE. Through knowing his way, Brother; and that here, always, he finds us.

MENDICANT. Lady—Lady! What is it, Lady? There's been something happening. Outside was a great crowd met me—pushing and pushing. I'd to hold on hard not to be trampled, and to get past them. What were they doing, Lady?

JUNIPER [*depressed by this symbol of the world's callousness.*] Forgetting! Forgetting the little Father—*burying* him!

MENDICANT. What was it, Lady? [CLARE *takes up earth, sprinkles it on his hand, makes the sign of the Cross on it, turns his hand, letting the earth fall.*] Oh? Some one dead? You mean—they are burying him?

[CLARE *moves his hand upward, then down, signifying 'yes.'*

97

JUNIPER. Look at that now! How have you told him? 'Tis a God's wonder his knowing it.

CLARE. He reads signs, Brother.

MENDICANT. Who was it? Some great lord; eh!—
[CLARE, *holding his hand, again signs by a side-way motion which means ' no.' Instinctively while doing so she shakes her head.*

MENDICANT. No? Nor rich? [*Again the motion.*] Not rich—poor? [*This time the sign is ' yes.'*] What was all the crowd, then? [CLARE *lays her hand on his heart, making there the sign of the Cross.*] You mean, *a good* man, Lady? But was that why there was a crowd? [*She signs ' yes.'*] So? Truly then, for such a crowd as that, and a *poor* man— 'twas a great wonder.

JUNIPER. Oh, hark now! He 's telling the truth —not for having seen it!

MENDICANT. Good, and holy, and poor, was he? So that men thought him great? . . . One they loved, eh? . . . That I should have loved, too—if I 'd had eyes and ears for him.

JUNIPER [*drinking it in*]. Oh, Sister, Sister dear!

MENDICANT. There was one I *did* love, Lady—*one*. But he 's gone: doesn't come now—not for this long time. 'Twas he first brought me here, Lady. Did you know that? [CLARE *signs: apparently she did.*] Where is he now? . . . Gone? . . . Where? [*Again she gives the sign of death.*] Dead? Him that I never saw—but *shall*, when God brings us all to His peace. [*The bell is still tolling far away,* CLARE *and* JUNIPER *wait till the* MENDICANT *again speaks.*] How I came to love him, would you know, Lady? I, a blind beggar, sat at the gate, where I always sit.

One day a hand touched mine—a hand different
from all the rest. That hand gave me bread—just
like others, but it gave warmth, too—held, didn't
let go. Then on my blind eyes—he kissed me.
Always after that—when he came—I knew *him*.
There was no one ever touched, and held, like he
did : none kissed like he did. I 'd so lived, Lady,
I 'd left off loving—sight and sound gone, the world
was nothing to me—I 'd no friend. But when *he*
came—deaf and blind though I was—I loved *him*.
[CLARE *and* JUNIPER *are looking at each other. They
know.*] And now dead, you say ? So that 's why
he didn't come any more. Has he been dead long,
Lady ? [CLARE *signs.*] No ? Ah ! [*With that
cry of discovery comes understanding.*]

JUNIPER. Look at that ! Oh, he knows, Sister !
Now he knows !

MENDICANT. Dead ! Gone ! Met me—passed me
—and I didn't know ! Oh, if I could have touched
him for the last time ! Who he was I shall never
know. But God knows ! One day he let me touch
his face—couldn't tell what like he was ; but there,
in my hands, I had, that once, the face of him I
loved. And that day I named him that had no
name—for *me*. ' The little Father ' I called him.

[JUNIPER *kneels, and lays his head on the*
MENDICANT'S *knee.*

JUNIPER. Oh, little Father, little Father ! Deaf
and blind ! Deaf and blind as I am, reach down
now, and give me thy blessing !

MENDICANT. Who—who is it ? What are ye
doing to me ? [JUNIPER'S *tears fall on his hands.*]
Crying ? What for ? For him ? So you loved

him too, eh ? Knew—heard—saw—dead to both of us now. But your love that knew him is no greater than mine. Face I never saw ! Voice I never heard ! But he touched me, and I loved *him*.

[JUNIPER *puts his arms round the* MENDICANT.

JUNIPER. You can't hear, and you can't see ! But you 've made *me*, Brother ! [*He kisses him.*] This for remembrance.

[*He draws back, the* MENDICANT *reaches up and feels his face ; a look of joy comes to him ; in a voice trembling with emotion he speaks.*

MENDICANT. Still alive ! Still alive ! Still alive !

JUNIPER. You hear that, Sister ? The little Father ' still alive ! '

[*He turns to* CLARE, *who stands looking on, the desire she had for him satisfied. The bell tolls on, but* JUNIPER *no longer hears it.*

CURTAIN

JUNIPER'S MIRACLE

It is the Feast of our Lady of the Angels; and in her new chapel at Portiuncula, candles lighted on the altar send out a cheerful radiance, which falls immediately on the rapt and upturned face of BROTHER JUNIPER. *The picture, or statue, upon which he gazes cannot be seen; in its recess above the altar it receives and gives back the light of its many candles; and a similar exchange appears to be taking place between it and* BROTHER JUNIPER. *Lost to the world—his job forgotten—he stands trailing the broom with which he has been sweeping the chapel; and might indefinitely so remain, but for the entry of* BROTHER JEROME, *who, as he passes across, turns on him a look of reproach, and failing from behind to catch the requisite attention, claps his hands smartly, and speaks.*

JEROME. The floor doesn't sweep *itself*, Brother!

JUNIPER [*meekly*]. No, Brother.

    [*He comes out of his reverie to resume sweeping; and* BROTHER JEROME, *having seen him to it, goes his way. Scarcely has he started again when the head comes off the broom.* JUNIPER *stops, and regards it as a misfortune which somehow he has deserved.*

JUNIPER. There! Now you 've done it!

    [*His view of the matter seems to find support from the altar.*

Yes, Lady; I was thinking that myself: we *are* just alike now, aren't we—him and me? Brother Broom 's lost his head, so what 's the good of him? And when I put it on him again—see!—it won't stay on. [*Broom-head in hand he demonstrates.*] Mine stays on, but loses itself, once I start thinking with it; his comes off when I start sweeping with it. For why then? . . . Let 's look! . . . Ah! 'Tisn't his head's fault, Lady; his neck 's broken. And I might have had as good a reason for being off with mine, had I ever been hanged by it. But I never was. Ought I to have been, Lady? Maybe that way I 'd have done God a better service than by keeping my head like it is now.

[*And now having something to narrate, he seats himself on a bench.*

I saw a man hanged once, Lady! I was sorry for him—very sorry; but I was glad it wasn't *me*. Blessed Lady, was that wrong? Tell me now—is it any use being sorry for a man if you aren't ready to take his pains for him? Being truly sorry means you 'd like *his* sorrow to be *your* sorrow—doesn't it, Lady? For isn't that how you felt under the Cross when Our Lord was dying for us? You wished it then, Lady, didn't you? Like a sword in your own heart that was. And God helping me, I 'd have wished it too, had I been there. Then why didn't I wish 'twas myself being hanged instead of the man I was sorry for? . . . Oh, why is there so much wickedness in me? For though the man they hanged wasn't the dear Lord Himself, hasn't He said—'Done to the least of these' (which means anybody), 'ye 've done it to Me'? . . . And,

Lady, could one do a better thing in this world
than take Our Lord down from the Cross, and put
ourselves instead of Him—bearing His pains for
Him ? . . . But you wanted to do it, and couldn't ;
so how can we—except for others ? Ah ! I might
have done it—*that* way. We might all be doing it
that way—for *others* !

    [*He pauses ; a new thought strikes him ; or does
       word come from the altar ?*

Prayer ? . . . ah, prayer 's one way of doing it. . . .
That 's what the little Father did, while he was in
life, didn't he ? . . . What 's he doing now, Lady ?
There you are ; but where is he ? You see him,
don't you, Lady. Every day ? . . . Is it when you
get up, or when you go to bed, or when ? Surely
you and he must be having great talks together.
. . . You love him, Lady ? Ah ! but you can't love
him more than *I* do : not *more*, only better—differently, more holily—not needing him like I do. Aye !
if I didn't need the little Father, I 'd not need
anything.

    Enter BROTHER ANGELO, *who first genuflects to
       the altar, then speaks.*

ANGELO. Brother Juniper.

JUNIPER [*defensively taking up the decapitated
broom, as an excuse for apparent idleness*]. Yes,
Brother ?

ANGELO. When you have finished here, Father
Minister wants you to mend these shoes for him.

JUNIPER [*taking and laying them down*]. Aye,
when I 'm finished here—what I 'm doing now—I
will, Brother.

ANGELO. And what are you doing now? You don't look very busy.

JUNIPER. But I am, Brother; for I'm trying to sweep up with a broom that's got no head to it. [*He shows it.*] How'll I do it?

ANGELO [*taking a knife from his girdle after inspecting the broom*]. Here is a knife, Brother. The handle wants shaping again.

JUNIPER. Aye. Now the Lord reward you for finding that out for me!

ANGELO. You could have done that for yourself, Brother.

JUNIPER. So I did: but not having a knife, where was the use?

ANGELO. Well, now you have it: so don't go wasting more time!

JUNIPER. No, Brother, I won't.

ANGELO [*turning as he departs*]. And the shoes, Brother: remember!

[*He is gone.* JUNIPER *does not bestir himself.*

JUNIPER. 'Wasting time'? He wouldn't have said 'wasting time' if he'd known it was you I was talking to—would he, Lady? When Father Minister sent me in to sweep here this morning, I wondered would I, maybe, get word with you, or sign—like Brother Conrad did—but not expecting it, Lady, any more than he did. And then, when the head of my broom came off, and I saw you smile, 'Ah!' thought I, ''tisn't only Brother Conrad, then, she's got an eye for, to care about!' You care for all of us, don't you, Lady?—and a God's wonder that is, we being all such sinners. But the little Father took our love to you, didn't he? When

104

he was dying, I said to him one day—' Give our Lady my love,' I said. And I know he 'd never forget a thing like that—though it wasn't on holy obedience that I told him. So since he died there 's no one been kinder to us than you 've been—no one : looking after every one of us, even when we are not looking after ourselves.

[*Rather forgetfully as he talks,* JUNIPER *repairs the broom handle, but he never finishes it.*

And I wonder, now, did he tell you of us each one by name, or only in the ruck like ? Eh, no matter. There you are, and here are we ; and we never forget each other, do we ? . . . And how 's the Holy Child to-day, Lady ? Is He well ? 'Tis a wonder He wasn't frightened, coming back into the world like you let Him the other day. Aye, Brother Conrad has told us of the holy charity you did for him then —when, being tempted of the Devil, he got up from his bed and came here to tell you of it : and how, after he 'd prayed three mortal hours, and hard put to it to keep awake, you stooped down, Lady, and gave the Holy Child into his arms for to kiss and be comforted. . . . It 's done him a world of good, Lady, that has—and me too. For never does he tire now of telling it, nor I of hearing it. Aye ! wasn't it wonderful ?

[*Gazing up with tender wistfulness,* JUNIPER *appears to see indications which frighten him. In panic-stricken haste he disclaims the honour She may be intending him.*

No, I 'm not asking, Lady, I 'm not asking you should ever do the like of that to me ! Eh ! wouldn't I be frightened if you did—for fear I should drop and be the killing of Him !—and always ever after be pointed at for it in Purgatory—and the last to get out for the same reason—' There goes the man that dropped the Holy Child ! ' Lord ! but it frightens me to think of it ! For didn't even holy St. Christopher find the weight of Him almost more than he could bear : and he big and strong as a giant, but me only a poor shoemaker. [*This reference to shoes reminds him of what he still has in his lap.*] Yes, Father Minister, I 'll remember ! [*Laying them down, he continues.*] . . . Lady, there 's something troubling me I can't understand. Here are you, and here am I ; but last week, when I went to Orvieto, you were there too ; and wherever I went there you were, Lady—like Our Lord Himself : for we know that, being God, He must be everywhere. But, Lady, how *you* do it too, is a God's wonder to me—listening to all so many at once ! How do you remember to sort out right all the things we go asking you ?—so many, and all so different ? And often you keep us waiting for them (don't you, Lady ?), which is good for us. But it 's a wonder you don't forget sometimes, and send the wrong things to the wrong people. Suppose, now, Father Elias goes asking you for more money for that big church he 's building over the bones of our little Father—though *he* didn't want it, did he, Lady ?— And suppose you sent along some poor holy beggars instead, who wanted some for themselves : would that be in answer to his prayer, Lady ? And would he thank you for it, do you think : or would he have it 'twas just a trick to teach him ? . . . Lady dear, what are you laughing for ? [*He gets a little scared*

106

as the thought comes to him.]   Are you going to play a trick on *me* ?   Are you going to give *me* something *I* didn't ask for ?   No, no, Holy Mother !   D'ye really mean it ?   Name o' Jesus !   God o' Mercy ! Suppose I were to drop Him ! ... Well, it 's you ought to know best ;   but I 've warned you. . . . Aye, for a minute, Lady ;   only for a minute !   And pray God I don't wake Him, and He start crying to go back to you again :   break my heart for me, that would !

> [*So saying he advances with arms crooked, and a face of sweet ecstasy, and receives what Our Lady wishes him to receive :   and is so standing when the bell sounds for the Angelus.   He kneels, and unable to cross himself in the ordinary way, makes the sign of the Cross with arms crooked under their imaginary burden ;   then very devoutly recites the Angelus in Latin.*

Ave Maria, gratiae plena, etc.

> [*Rising again, he suddenly remembers, and stands faced with a dilemma for the solution of which he turns again to the altar.*

Eh !   And now it 'll be our feeding time.   Did you know, Lady, that we always eat at noon, with the Angelus put in first to give us an appetite ?   [*A bell starts clanging.*]   There it is now !   And I ought to be going, Lady.   If I don't, they 'll be after me.

> [*At this moment* BROTHER ANGELO *hurries in, pressed for time, carrying a fresh supply of candles, with which—after genuflection—he replaces those which have burnt out.* JUNIPER *stands looking on with crooked arms.   Other*

Brothers *are now following their appetites with speed, past the open entrance to the chapel.*

ANGELO [*as he starts on the candles*]. Do you not hear the bell, Brother ?

JUNIPER. Yes, Brother.

ANGELO. It 's refectory. Be quick and finish, or you will be late.

JUNIPER. Yes, Brother.

ANGELO [*looking round as he plies his job*]. What are you holding your arms like that for ?

JUNIPER [*with an apologetic glance to the altar, for so putting it*]. I 've had it put on me for a penance.

ANGELO [*coming down, surprised*]. Oh ? By whom.

JUNIPER. I put it on myself—for holy obedience.

ANGELO. Don't be foolish, Brother. Put them down !

JUNIPER. I can't—till I 'm free of it, Brother.

ANGELO. Then how are you going to eat anything ?

JUNIPER. I don't know—hadn't thought; maybe I 'll go without.

ANGELO [*who is a stickler for the rules*]. And have you Father Minister's permission to go without ?

JUNIPER. No, Brother : only my own.

[ANGELO *raises his meek eyebrows, but for the moment says nothing. He genuflects to the altar, then says, as he turns to go :*

ANGELO. You would not be doing this if Father Elias were here, Brother.

JUNIPER. No, I shouldn't have begun doing it.

ANGELO [*drily.*] *God* sees you, Brother.

[*So saying he departs.*

108

JUNIPER. But *he* didn't see what I 've got here, did he, Lady ?—Didn't see anything. . . . Am I to go now ; or will you have me stay ? Is it just for my own dinner I must be leaving Him ? . . . What for are you laughing now ?

[*He hears footsteps approaching.*

Oh, here 's some one coming to fetch me ! Take Him back, Lady ! Take Him back, for the love of God ! Else I 'll not know what to do with Him, nor with myself either. Quick, Lady !

[*Hurriedly he makes the restoration that his play-acting requires of him, just as* FATHER MATTEO *enters from behind.*

MATTEO [*in a kindly puzzled tone*]. Brother Juniper, who were you talking to ?

JUNIPER. Maybe it was only to myself, Father.

MATTEO. No, no : it was not to yourself, Juniper. You don't say ' Lady ' to yourself. Where *is* the Lady ? . . . On holy obedience, Brother, answer me !

[JUNIPER *stands stripped of disguise. Heaven has dropped him to earth. He owns up.*

JUNIPER. She 's up yonder. I was only just making belief that Our Lady 'd been talking to me. Was it wrong, Father dear ?

[FATHER MATTEO *is not quite as shocked as his words seem to indicate ; but he does his duty.*

MATTEO. Very wrong, Brother. Proud, vain-glorious, presumptuous.

JUNIPER [*dimly at a loss*]. Me proud, eh ? I 've got to it at last, then. . . . But Father, we talk to *her*, don't we ? We are told to.

MATTEO. We *pray* to her, Brother.

JUNIPER. Yes, Father; and she answers. Else we wouldn't do it, would we, Father?

MATTEO. We do not *hear* her answer, Brother.

JUNIPER. No, Father; but sometimes we see it, or find it, maybe, where we didn't look for it. For while we thought it would be outside somewhere, there it was *in* us all the time—in our hearts, Father.

[MATTEO, *perceiving that more is to come, sits down and resigns himself to the situation.*

MATTEO. Well, Brother?

JUNIPER. And isn't that what's called having faith, Father?

MATTEO. Why yes, Brother. What then?

JUNIPER [*much relieved*]. Well, Father, I've always had it there—in my heart, like we all do, and think nothing of it but to be thankful. And I was only for having it in my ears as well. But I wasn't proud of 'em, Father!—not proud like the deaf adder that stopped hers, so she shouldn't hear anything she didn't like. But if it's proud to shut 'em, and proud to open 'em, then you can't do anything with your ears at all, except just wag 'em like donkeys do. But if I'm right to have faith in my heart, why am I wrong to have faith in my ears, Father?

MATTEO. Because, Brother, in so doing you have presumed that God, for a miserable thing like you, was working wonders.

JUNIPER. But He always is, Father.

MATTEO. A miracle, I mean.

JUNIPER. And isn't it a miracle—we such sinners—that our prayers are ever answered, Father?

MATTEO. That is by God's grace, Brother.

JUNIPER. And isn't God's grace a miracle, Father?

MATTEO [*who is not above learning from* JUNIPER]. Yes, Brother. [*He sits meditative.*]

JUNIPER [*anxious*]. You don't mind me asking you, Father—things I'm not clear about?

MATTEO. No, no, Brother.

[*He draws* JUNIPER *to sit beside him.*

JUNIPER. Father, here I've lived, fifty years and more: and except when I've sinned, there's nothing I've ever done that wasn't a miracle: God's doing, not mine. Sure 'twas a miracle brought me to the little Father; and a miracle how ever he managed to find a use for me! But he did, Father, didn't he? Aye, a great miracle that was; and his soul resting in glory now.

MATTEO [*laying his hand on* JUNIPER]. The miracle is still going on, Brother . . . but so is dinner. You mustn't forget that.

JUNIPER. No, Father.

MATTEO. Let us say a prayer together, Juniper: and then we will go in—with the others.

JUNIPER. Yes, Father.

[*They kneel, cross themselves, and pray silently—*
JUNIPER *with lips that move to the words.*
FATHER MATTEO, *again crossing himself, rises first. He genuflects to the altar with the slow heavy movements of old age, then goes.* JUNIPER, *conscious, without turning his head, that he is now alone, becomes audible in prayer.*

JUNIPER. Gate of Life, Way to Jesus, Virgin pure without sin, Holy Mother of God, pray for me!

[*He rises.*] And next time you are up in Heaven, Lady, you 'll give my love to the little Father, won't you ?

> [*The look he receives seems to satisfy him ; with a nod of friendly understanding, he turns to go —then, remembering what is proper, makes a knee of it. He is almost out of the chapel when he calls to mind something he was forgetting. He returns, gathers up broom-head and handle, and the shoes from the bench where he has laid them.*

JUNIPER. Yes, Father dear. There ! I 've remembered. [*And off he goes to dinner.*

CURTAIN

NOTE

The candles of which Angelo brings a fresh supply, are small ones, set in a 'hearse' on a lower level below the large ones which make a row on the super-altar. Of these only the end one (or two) can be seen by the audience.

THE TEMPTATION OF JUNIPER

 *A large cell ; on one side a door, on the other (to the right) a big chest ; to the left a table and bench, beyond them a bed at centre. Between the door and the bed is a narrow recess covered by a curtain. It is night ; from the ceiling hangs a small lamp which gives but a dim light ; there are also candles in rough iron sockets. A group of the Brothers are in process of disrobing themselves of mummer's attire, which they strew on table and bench, while another folds and lays them piece by piece in the chest. As they put off their mummings, they resume their friars' robes. BROTHER GILES, who is not one of them, stands hearing the news.*

CONRAD. Oh, it 's a great sight we 'll give them at the Feast, Brother. And none has yet seen any of it but ourselves.

JEROME. There on his throne sits Brother Angelo, for God the Father, bright and shining, with all his angels round him ; and then, in comes Brother Simon, dressed like the Devil, with flames after him.

PACIFICO. The very sight of him, Brother Giles, makes you cross yourself and tremble !

GILES. But is it with permission ? Does Father Minister Elias know all this ?

CONRAD. Why, yes, Brother ; 'twas by his order. ' You must have a Devil in the play,' he says.

113

' God 'll never frighten them enough,' he says, ' unless He 's got the Devil to help Him.'

GILES. Will he be back for it ?

JEROME. He comes to-morrow, Brother.

PACIFICO. All this stuff and treasure was of his
getting. [*Giving up his robe.*] Lay it in, Brother !

Enter RUFUS *hastily, followed by* SIMON *dressed as the
Devil, concealed under cloak and hood. When
presently he discloses himself suited in black goat-
skin, with horrid glittering eyes, he is truly enough
to frighten anybody.*

RUFUS. In here, Brother, in here ! Has any one
seen you ?

SIMON. Only Brother Humble at the gate. I
opened to him—so [*he throws back his hood, and pulls
open his robe*], gave him one whisk of my tail, one
gleam of my eyes : he 's lying there on his belly still,
screaming himself dead, I shouldn't wonder.

PACIFICO. Take it off, Brother ! Take it off !
The Devil himself couldn't look worse.

SIMON. Not yet. Where is Brother Juniper ? Does
he know of this ?

RUFUS. He knows nothing. He has only just
returned from a journey. Why ?

SIMON. Ah, then we 've got him ! Juniper said
a man had no reason to fear the Devil, so long
as he wasn't in mortal sin himself. I want to
try him.

GILES. What would you do, Brother ?

SIMON. Make him give himself up for lost, and run
away from me.

GILES. And if he doesn't, Brother ?

SIMON. Then I'll cook my tail, and eat it! Where is he?

RUFUS. In the refectory, breaking bread; his first for three days.

SIMON. When he's done eating, I'll see him.

GILES. Not to-night, Brother; he is weary.

SIMON. The best time for trying him.

GILES [*resignedly*]. Very well, Brother.

SIMON. Brother Giles, what do you promise me that he runs not at first sight of me?

GILES. Charge him to keep here on holy obedience —then he will not.

JEROME. We'll do that: tell him 'tis at the bidding of Father Elias—his orders waiting for him.

> [*The listening* Brothers *warm to the plot; chuckles go round. Presently all are in it, except* GILES.

SIMON [*to* GILES]. Well? Now, then. What?

GILES. I will give you all my meat at the Feast, Brother, if he runs against holy obedience. Also a thousand Aves that you may be forgiven, should there be sin in what you are doing.

SIMON. And the same for you, if I fail.

GILES [*as he goes out*]. Do not trouble, Brother.

SIMON [*calling after him*]. And you won't tell Juniper, now!

GILES [*looking in again*]. No, Brother.

> [*He goes.*

SIMON. Now, then; clear the ground! Hide where you shall not be seen! No noise, no laughing! Jerome, bring Juniper!

> [JEROME *and the rest go out.*

Nay, not too much light, though: just enough

for him to see by. [*He puts out the candles.
Two of the* Brothers *creep in, laughing.*] Quick, in
with you! If coming he sees you, you spoil all.
[*They retire.*] Now! [*He puts out the last candle.*]
Sharpen your legs for a run, Juniper! You'll need
them.

> [*Still wearing his cloak loose about him, he
> goes and hides in the recess. Enter* JEROME,
> *followed by* JUNIPER.*

JEROME. Come in, Brother; you must be weary.

JUNIPER. I am, Brother; and it's my bed I'll be
going to. What am I wanted here for?

JEROME. You are to sleep here.

JUNIPER. Here? Not in that bed: that's where
Father Elias sleeps.

JEROME. Father Elias is away, Brother.

JUNIPER. Oh! Did he say I was to sleep here?

JEROME. You *are* to sleep here, Brother.

JUNIPER. Not if I get thinking about him in the
same bed, I shan't.

JEROME. He will not be in the same bed, Brother.

JUNIPER. No, but has been, and will again. I
don't like the look of it.

JEROME. Too hard for you?

JUNIPER. Hard? It's my head's too soft and
weak to lie where his does. Once I get dreaming
of him, you'll all wake to hear me screaming for
mercy.

JEROME. Very well; scream, Brother!

JUNIPER [*backing to the door*]. Ah! I'll be going.

JEROME. On holy obedience, Brother, do as you
are told. In that chest things of the Community's
are lying, which need to be guarded.

JUNIPER. That's not the rule Father Francis made for us. We were to guard nothing—except ourselves from the Devil.

JEROME. It is the rule now, Brother.

JUNIPER [*with a sigh of dejection*]. Aye!

JEROME. So now they are in your charge; see that you do not lose them. Good-night, Brother Juniper. Sleep well.

[*He goes to the door, which, standing ajar, he finds encumbered with the crouching bodies of the listening* Brothers. *Stepping over them, and leaving the door rather more ajar than before, he joins the throng.* JUNIPER *has turned from the chest to the bed, and stands regarding it with disfavour.*

JUNIPER. Oh, Lord! Is it there I must be all this blessed night? 'Sleep here,' he said; but not in the bed, he didn't tell me I had to.

[*He returns to the chest, considers it, then spreads his cloak on it.*

Sure, if what's in here wants guarding, and I sleep on it—them that want to steal it will have to steal me too.

[*He kneels, and crosses himself.*

Holy Jesus, Maker of men, Shepherd of sheep, Saviour of sinners, Comforter of fools, Lover of our little Father Francis—to Thy taking, to Thy keeping; for making, for reaping; for mending or breaking; watching or sleeping—let all bodies and souls be made Thine, at the last Day's waking. Amen. . . . God bless Father Elias, and keep him safe for ever, and away from me this night. Amen.

[*He rises.*

There : now that 's done—God come and put me
to bed, so I 'll not be afraid of him !

    [*He goes to the lamp, and is about to put it out,
       then stops.*

No ; you stay, Brother ! You stay, till you hear
me asleep.

    [*He stretches himself on the chest, and draws the
       cloak around him. There is a pause. The*
       Brothers *at the prayer of* JUNIPER *have left
       off laughing ; but they still wait, expectant.
       Presently with hood and cloak loose, ready to
       disclose himself,* SIMON *emerges from his
       hiding-place, standing back where the light is
       dim. He starts whinnying like a goat. After
       one or two repetitions,* JUNIPER *becomes aware
       of it, and half sits up. From the darkness
       across the room comes a voice silky and
       secretive ; and (for dramatic purposes) it is
       the* DEVIL *who is now speaking.*

DEVIL. Brother Juniper.

JUNIPER [*startled, trying to see*]. In God's name,
who are you ?

    DEVIL. One you know well, Juniper.

                [JUNIPER *starts crossing himself.*

JUNIPER. Name o' Jesus !

DEVIL. No : name ' Satan,'—commonly called
' Devil.'

    [JUNIPER, *springing from the chest to the wall-
       side, kneels, and raising the lid towards him as
       a shield, starts praying. It is a queer jumble
       of words—the ' Lord's Prayer ' and the ' Ave
       Maria ' combined ; and now in Latin, now in
       the common tongue, he stumbles precipitately*

along the only path to salvation he knows. The DEVIL (*it isn't fair, for by all the rules this should have put him to flight*) *watches him, undismayed and unmoved. And as the prayer seems like continuing, he interrupts it.*

DEVIL. When you have *quite* done praying, Juniper !

JUNIPER. Which I haven't ! In God's name, be off with you !

DEVIL. I don't do anything in God's name.

[*This lights a spark :* JUNIPER *lets down the lid.*

JUNIPER. Oh, don't you ? That's all *you* know !

DEVIL. What do I ? Tell me !

[JUNIPER *finds a danger in talking to the* DEVIL, *unless he is also talking to God at the same time. And so, from now on, beneath his controversy with the Evil One, runs a swift under-current of ejaculatory appeals for Divine aid.*

JUNIPER. Everything ! (O Lord, help me to teach him, the poor thing he is ! God be merciful !) You suffer . . . you burn, you are miserable, you stink —all in God's name. It's in God's name you are as ugly as you are ! It's in God's name you make men hate you, and be afraid of you.

DEVIL. Do *you* hate me ?

[*At this terrifying question, the conscience-stricken* JUNIPER *begins praying again, very fast beneath his breath.*

JUNIPER. Oh, God be merciful ! God be merciful ! Merciful God, am I to tell him the truth ?

DEVIL [*insistently*]. *Do* you hate me, Juniper ?

JUNIPER. No, but in God's name I'm sorry for you.

DEVIL. Why ?

JUNIPER. Because you can never come to anything but a bad end.

DEVIL [*with easy assurance*]. Not yet.

JUNIPER. You have—*here*.

DEVIL. How here ?

JUNIPER. Sure, I 'm bad end enough for you ! (God be merciful !) You can't make me worse than I am already.

DEVIL. I 'm not so sure, Brother.

JUNIPER. Eh. But *I* am. And when you go——

DEVIL. Aye—*when*. But for all your praying you haven't got rid of me yet.

JUNIPER. No ; and (God be merciful !) I 've left off praying for it. I did at first : any one would—left with his senses—at the mere sight of you. I 'd not have ye to go, now; I 'd have ye stay.

DEVIL. Then, why, at first, did you tell me to go ?

JUNIPER. ' In God's name,' I said : meaning, if it was His will. So now, in God's name, I tell you to stay.

DEVIL. Why, now ?

JUNIPER. Because here (God be merciful !) while you 're wasting your time tempting me, you 're saving others ; doing a good work in spite of yourself.

DEVIL. Oh, there 's many will run to sin without *me* to fetch them !

JUNIPER. Eh ? Then you 're not as important as you make out : and (God be merciful !) He 's letting you know it. You 'll learn the truth about yourself some day.

DEVIL. The truth, eh ? Well, what is it ?

JUNIPER. The last thing *you* 'd ever be thinking !
Aye ! if you 'd even seen yourself as you *are*, you 'd
go and drown yourself. And a good end to you
that would be, and a merciful, if there was water
enough to do it.

DEVIL. Water, with me in it ? Fire and water
don't mix, Juniper !

JUNIPER. So you 'd rather roast, would you ?
It 's a poor choice you have. (God be merciful !)
And it 's *you*, making yourself out to be somebody,
and us thinking it, does all the mischief. Years
back, I used to be so afraid of you I couldn't stir
out after dark—couldn't go to bed alone ; so had
to marry a wife—God being merciful ; though, at
the time it didn't seem like it. For, after a year
of me—God being merciful—she died : and a saving
for both of us that was ; for it took her to Heaven,
and me to the little Father.

DEVIL. The little Father ? Who is he ?

JUNIPER. One you 've tried tempting, many 's the
time ; and now gone to his glory. And if you look
round on yourself for your blackest bruises—there 's
where the little Father has set his mark on you.

DEVIL [*appearing to look*]. I don't find them,
Brother.

JUNIPER. Ah ! It 's your hairiness that 's hiding
'em, then ! Do you never moult ? Ah ! then 'ud be
the time for you to repent and get rid of yourself—
being a bit less ugly, and nearer to Heaven maybe,
then, than you are now—God being merciful !

DEVIL. Maybe not, Brother : but maybe nearer
to you—' God being merciful.' For if I wasn't so
hairy, you might not know me so easily.

JUNIPER. Ah! but I 'd never mistake ye, God helping me; not till those horns came off.

DEVIL. You seem very safe and sure of yourself, Juniper.

JUNIPER. I 'm not sure of myself; but I 'm sure of the little Father. The little Father, he says to me, ' You needn't be afraid of anything—so long as you fear God and love Him.' ' But if you don't fear God,' he says, ' you must fear the Devil : it 's one or other.' I made the choice then, Brother ; and it wasn't you. And if there 's one left in the world that I 'm still afraid of, he 's not you, nor anything a bit like you.

DEVIL. Of a truth, Brother, *do* you not fear me ?

JUNIPER [*a little scared, for the* DEVIL'S *voice is not pleasant*]. God be merciful ! No . . . in my flesh, I do ; but not in my heart and soul, I don't—God and the little Father helping me.

[*Whereat the* DEVIL *makes a move towards him.*

JUNIPER. Ah, now, don't you come too near, or I shall bite you !

DEVIL. I will ask you one question, Juniper ! Would you rather be damned yourself, or have others damned for you ?

JUNIPER [*after a long pause*]. Why for me ? If I 'm not to be damned, there 's no reason for any to be.

DEVIL. But some *will* be damned. Don't you know it, Juniper ?

JUNIPER. I 'm not sure, Brother. (God be merciful!) Damnation is only what *you* promise 'em : that dish is *your* making, not God's. And you being a liar, you 'll break your word yet, God helping you. (God be merciful!) . . . Nobody 's quite damned so long as there 's *one* prays for him. And I 'll never leave off praying, not for anybody.

DEVIL. Do you pray—for *me*, Juniper?

JUNIPER. Aye, but I don't let Father Elias hear tell of it.

DEVIL. And if Father Elias told you, on holy obedience, *not* to pray for me, Juniper—what should you do then?

JUNIPER. If he was to tell me that, I 'd know it was *your* doing; and turning it to prayer for *him* 'ud be the same thing. I 'd be praying you out of bad ways still.

DEVIL. You answer well: you are clever, Juniper.

JUNIPER. Clever? Did you ever try to sharpen a cow's tail on a pea-stick? When you 've done it, and haven't repented trying it, call me clever for telling you.

DEVIL. Repent, eh? How would you make me repent?

JUNIPER. I wouldn't try, Brother. (God be merciful!)

DEVIL. But when you pray for me, do you not pray for my repentance?

JUNIPER. No, Brother.

DEVIL. What, then?

JUNIPER. That you may find out you are nothing.

DEVIL. Nothing.

JUNIPER. Aye—that you may lose yourself.

DEVIL. Explain, Juniper.

JUNIPER. Where 'd you be, if there was no sin— so you could tempt nobody?

DEVIL. More in Hell than ever, Brother.

JUNIPER. But what 'ud Hell be to you, with only yourself in it ?

DEVIL. Still Hell.

JUNIPER. Just your own silly face in a dirty pool —and you looking for it, till—with your self grown so small—there 'd be nothing left worth looking for —God being merciful.

DEVIL. That may be : *but not yet !* There is still something of me left. Hell has still room in it for others. There is room in it for *you*, Juniper !

[*Whereupon he advances toward the terrified* JUNIPER, *who backs to the wall, then slips aside, with the* DEVIL *after him. There is a whispered gabble of voices at the door*—' Leave it ! Clear the way ! Now he 's going to run.' *They give a push and depart : the door swings slowly open.* JUNIPER's *way of escape lies clear. But* JUNIPER, *now prayerfully perambulating the room with the* DEVIL *after him, does not heed it.*

JUNIPER. God be merciful ! God be merciful ! God be merciful ! As it was in the beginning is now and ever shall be, world without end, Amen !

[*Round table, under table, over bed, back he comes upon the chest again. Seizing the cord handle, he lifts the lid, leaps in, pulls it down, and holds it fast. The game is up. Rejecting the open door,* JUNIPER *has stuck to his post. From outside comes the laughter of the* Brothers.

DEVIL [*rebukingly*]. Ssh !

[*Crossing to the door he resumes cowl and habit.*

124

DEVIL. Brother Juniper . . . Brother Juniper
. . . Brother Juniper . . . On holy obedience
come forth, for I would speak with you.

[*Cautiously* JUNIPER *lifts the lid, and puts out
a nose.*

JUNIPER. Eh ? Who—who is ca—— ?

DEVIL. You have done well—you have answered
well, Brother, so for the present shall not be damned
—'God being merciful.' What you have said is
true : save for a weakness of the flesh, you fear not
the Devil. . . . But I am *not* the Devil.

JUNIPER [*rising and getting out*]. Then who the
Devil are you ?

DEVIL [*having his last fling*]. I am FATHER
MINISTER ELIAS ! [*So saying, he goes. In abject
terror,* JUNIPER *falls back into the chest, legs in air.*]

JUNIPER. Oh, Lord ! Holy Virgin and Saints !
Now I 've done for myself. 'Twas Father Elias set
a trap for me !

[*Suddenly the sound of inextinguishable laughter
strikes his ear. The listening* Brothers *are
enjoying themselves.* JUNIPER *listens, and
interprets to his better comfort.*

JUNIPER. Laughing ? What for are they laughing ? Eh ! They 'd not be all laughing like that,
if Father Elias was about.

[*Hope dawns in him. He gets up.*

JUNIPER. 'Twas the Devil, after all, then ! He 's
told me a lie. Praise be to God !

[*Weak and trembling, he sits down. And then
enter to him* BROTHERS JEROME, CONRAD, *and*
SIMON, *followed by* BROTHER GILES ; *at the door
stand other* Brothers.

JEROME. Brother Juniper, what was all that noise about ?   What is the matter ?

JUNIPER. I 've—I 've been seeing the Devil, Brother.

SIMON. Did he—frighten you, Brother ?

JUNIPER. Aye : he did that.   But he only did it by telling me he was Father Elias.

GILES. *Father Elias ?*

JUNIPER. 'Twasn't fair, was it, Brother ?

GILES. No, Brother.

JUNIPER. And, Brother dear, you 're *quite* sure, aren't you, that Father Elias hasn't come back to us, without our knowing it.

GILES. He has *not*, Brother.

JUNIPER. You 're all sure—every one of you ?

ALL. We are sure, Brother.

JUNIPER [*with a sigh of relief*]. Eh, then.   It *was* the Devil, after all.   God being merciful !

CURTAIN

THE ODOUR OF SANCTITY

In a corner of the wall, by the main gate of Spoleto, there is building. To the right stands the gate; to the left a large pile of stones; in between, still in course of erection, is scaffolding. From overhead hangs the rope of a crane. The ground is strewn with loose stone, piled planks, rubble and mortar. From the builders' platform, two Boys have lifted a loose plank, and are lowering it to the ground. Their work accomplished, they slide down the scaffolding, and are about to make off with their booty, when one of them looks round and starts.

1ST BOY. Hide it! Quick! Somebody's coming.

2ND BOY. He's all right. He's only an old beggar.

[*The* Boys *stand back,* JUNIPER *enters, dressed in rags, very footsore and weary.*

JUNIPER. Heigho! Is here a place where a sinner can sit down? God be good to me! If a seat were offered me in Hell now, I'd be tempted to take it.

1ST BOY [*anxious to be rid of him*]. Go inside, Gaffer, you'll find it better there.

JUNIPER. Will you *carry* me in?

1ST BOY. We can't carry *you.*

JUNIPER. You were carrying a plank bigger than me just now. Why?

2ND BOY. We wanted it.

JUNIPER. And you don't want *me,* eh? But as I

127

happen to want myself, you 'll have to put up with me. Eh, eh, eh!

[*Wincing painfully he sits down on a stone-pile.*

1st BOY [*sympathetically*]. You 've come a long way, Gaffer?

JUNIPER. Aye. I 've come from my cradle, and I 'm going to my grave. It 's the same journey for all. But to-day it 's been a bigger bit than most days.

2ND BOY. Where from, Mister?

JUNIPER. Perugia.

2ND BOY. Oh; that 's a long way!

1ST BOY. That 's where the holy man lives that 's coming to-day.

JUNIPER. Holy man? From Perugia? There 's no holy man in Perugia that I know. . . . What 's he coming here for?

1ST BOY. To preach.

JUNIPER. Oh! It 's his holiness the Bishop, you mean?

1ST BOY. No; this is one of the holy friars of St. Francis, that was made holy from knowing him; one that never sins, and does miracles. Brother Juniper, his name is.

JUNIPER. If I fall down, don't pick me up; just leave me. . . . How do you know he 's holy?

1ST BOY. They all say so; everybody knows it.

JUNIPER. Does *he*?

2ND BOY. If he doesn't, why 's he coming to preach?

JUNIPER. You 're right! 'Twas the Lord opened your mouth that time. Why does he?

2ND BOY. Some say as he 's only a fool——

JUNIPER. Ah! You 've wise men among you!

2ND BOY. And just pretending.

1ST BOY. But they are all waiting to see him.

2ND BOY. That's why they are up there on the wall now—because this is the way he'll come.

JUNIPER. And how'll they know him, when he does come?

1ST BOY. Because he's a holy friar, and wears the robe.

JUNIPER. Suppose he was to take it off, and come naked?

2ND BOY. He wouldn't be a holy man if he did that.

JUNIPER. You'll see him do it, then!

2ND BOY. I think you are funny.

JUNIPER. That's better than if you thought me holy. Yet there's been saints went naked when they'd a reason. Have ye never heard tell of St. Francis rolling in the snow, making himself a wife and five children all out of snowballs? Wasn't he naked then?

1ST BOY. Did they come alive?

JUNIPER. No. 'Tis of a temptation I'm telling you. And if you go tempting Brother Juniper, calling him holy when he comes, you'll see him run naked as a cat when a dog's after her. Holy! Do I look holy?

2ND BOY [giggling shyly]. No.

JUNIPER. And are you holy, little one?

2ND BOY. No.

JUNIPER. Why not? Why not? . . . Why aren't you?

1ST BOY. We've just stole a plank that isn't ours.

JUNIPER. What for?

1ST BOY. To make a swing of.

2ND BOY. A see-saw, he means.

JUNIPER. But won't you put it back when you've done?

1ST BOY. We shan't have time. When them it belongs to come back, we shall run away.

JUNIPER. Where are they now ?

2ND BOY. Gone to dinner.

JUNIPER. And what 's all this here for ?

2ND BOY. They 're building.

JUNIPER. What ?

2ND BOY. Walls.

JUNIPER. What for ?

1ST BOY. Keep people out, I suppose.

JUNIPER. Keep 'em out ? Why d'you have gates to let 'em in, then ?

1ST BOY. But bad people, Master. You 've got to keep *them* out, haven't you ?

JUNIPER. That only makes 'em worse, little one. Letting 'em in 'ud make 'em better.

2ND BOY. Are you a bad person ?

JUNIPER. I am. You won't find a worse than me in the world. . . . But you 're not afraid of me.

2ND BOY. You aren't really bad; you 're only silly.

JUNIPER. Well ; isn't being bad the silliest thing in the world ?

2ND BOY. I don't know. Taking their planks, the builders call us bad names. We don't mind.

1ST BOY. If they could catch us, they'd beat us. But we aren't silly so long as we can run quicker, are we ?

JUNIPER. You can't run quicker than God, little one.

1ST BOY. God ? He don't mind our taking 'em.

JUNIPER. Ah ! You may be right ! Go on; have your swing, then ! and I 'll keep the look-out for you. But it 's no holy man, mind you, has told you to do that !

[*The* Boys *take him at his word, and balance the plank into position under the scaffolding.*

130

1ST BOY. He isn't silly; he's nice.

2ND BOY. Come on; you take that end!

> [*They begin swinging; and so continue at intervals, with occasional readjustment and exchange of ends.*

JUNIPER [*peering up at the people on the walls*]. So you're looking for a holy man, are ye? O Lord, here was sin turned to a blessing! If vanity hadn't made me change my clothes on the way, there'd a been worse temptation waiting for me here. Eh! That was a wise beggar told me his was the better suit. Was it the Lord Himself? I shouldn't wonder. Dear Lord, the trouble I am to 'ee!—always needing to be looked after and saved from sinful ways. What would I do the same minute, did He ever forget me? Holy! And I—that have come here to preach to them! How 'm I to do it, dear Lord? Show me how!

> [*He sits thinking; then begins to peel off his very ragged outer garment, exposing worse rags below.*

Aye, that's one way. Now show me another.

> [*As the cold air strikes him he shivers. A soberly-clad* CITIZEN, *coming from the city gate, stops to look at him.*

CITIZEN. You look cold, Brother.

JUNIPER. I look the truth; I *am* cold. And I've the right to be. I've the cold heart, full of wickedness.

CITIZEN. Change it, Brother.

JUNIPER. It's what I'm trying now—with a change of clothes to begin on.

CITIZEN. Were your others no better than these?

JUNIPER. Could they be better? Look—there!
and there, and there [*displaying the holes*]. Isn't
that daylight? And isn't the light God sends better
than man's makings?

CITIZEN. For clothes?

JUNIPER. Aye—for clothes.

CITIZEN. I should have said not.

JUNIPER. Then you 'd be a fool, Brother, like me.
I said ' not ' till I got these. They 've taught me.

CITIZEN [*seating himself*]. Aye? Taught you what?

JUNIPER. Wisdom. Oh! 'twas a wise man first
said that. ' Winter,' he said, ' is God's bakehouse.'

CITIZEN. ' Winter is God's bakehouse '?

JUNIPER. Aye; that seems silly, doesn't it?
Well, say it over and over till you seem silly yourself. Then you 've got it.

CITIZEN [*still exploring for its meaning*]. ' Winter is
God's bakehouse '!

JUNIPER. Aye. D'you not feel yourself silly yet?
Try again!

CITIZEN. You seem a merry kind of fellow.

JUNIPER. Merry! [*Then peeping in through the
holes in his rags.*] There, Brother! Did you hear
that?

CITIZEN. Who are you speaking to?

JUNIPER. My own body. When I got him in these
clothes an hour ago, he was as miserable as a flea on
a donkey's back that 's got no hair. Now he feels
better for it. Merry! Keep it up, Brother!

CITIZEN. But tell me, friend: ' Winter is God's
bakehouse '—what does it bake?

JUNIPER. Hearts . . . souls . . . insides: makes
'em wish they were warm, instead of the cold things

132

they are. Yes : I 'd the cold heart. Now this has taught me.

CITIZEN. Lend it to me, Brother.

JUNIPER. Lend it you ? And am I to go naked ?

CITIZEN. No, Brother. I will give you mine for it—this cloak.

JUNIPER. Do that : I might as well have kept my own !

CITIZEN. You are a strange fellow.

JUNIPER. And this—would you have worn it ?

CITIZEN. No, Brother, I would not. Yet would I gladly have seen you to a better one.

JUNIPER. Now was that kindness, or was that foolishness ? . . . I keep what I 've got, for fear of worse happening. . . . Did you ever hear of the wicked prophet who went off to preach for a king as the king wanted him to preach, and not as God wanted ? And went to it riding on an ass ?

CITIZEN. One named Balaam.

JUNIPER. Aye, sure. 'Twas he. And of how, all at once, the ass met an angel, and took fright of him ?

CITIZEN. Yes ; surely.

JUNIPER. And the ass starting to kick, and the prophet to swear, they made a match of it ; till the ass kicked so high he got his hind hoof hitched in the stirrup, and couldn't get it out. ' Lord love me,' says the prophet, ' if you 're going to get up, it 's time I got down ! ' So he did ; and that saved him. . . . What for are you laughing ?

CITIZEN. You would make any one laugh, I think. Who are you ?

JUNIPER. I mustn't tell you. There 's some looking for me, that I don't want to find me.

CITIZEN. Have you been doing something, Brother
—that you should not ?

JUNIPER. Aye ; many times ; but not that !
Holy ? The Lord forbid !

CITIZEN. I don't understand. Holy, you say ?

JUNIPER. If *I* was holy, there 'd be nothing in it.
If I was wise, where 'd wisdom be in the world ?
Am I beautiful ? I 'd bite my head off before I 'd
believe it.

CITIZEN. Has any one been calling you beautiful ?

JUNIPER. They 've been calling me worse. That 's
why I don't tell you who I am. You might be one
of 'em.

CITIZEN. Indeed, no, Brother. I should not, from
the look of you, say you were either wise, or beautiful, or holy. Yet wisdom and beauty and holiness
may all be in you.

JUNIPER. Don't ! You frighten me !

CITIZEN. Even as good corn has root in muddy
earth ; and the muddier it be, the better the corn
grows.

JUNIPER. Eh ! That 's true. Mud 's what I am.
A muck-heap. But 'twas God made me. And
when He made the whole world, wasn't it mud too ?
—till He made things grow from it : flowers, and
fruit, and birds ; and then came Adam, and little
children, and men with hearts to love each other—
better than they could love themselves.

CITIZEN. That is true. Go on, Brother !

JUNIPER. Listen ; I 'll tell you a secret. Mud
and corn, you said. There lived a man once—dead
now : God has lifted him to glory—came and set his
mark on me—and on others. There I watched him

grow; God gave me eyes for that, Brother. I was only mud: but his feet left their print on me. And it's mud I still am—just for the showing of feet, marked like his feet. And now that's the trouble; because he left me his mark, they think I'm holy. Isn't it awful—me, the mud I am, for any one to call holy?

CITIZEN. The Lord so bless and keep you, Brother. For though I know not who you are—though I may guess—I know surely of whom you speak—our little Father—the Blessed Francis of Assisi.

JUNIPER. Aye; the little Father, the little Father! . . . Did you know—did you ever see him, Brother?

CITIZEN. No, Brother.

JUNIPER. But are you not one of us?

CITIZEN. Only a Tertiary, Brother. I am of the world still; yet he is my Father.

JUNIPER. All the world's Father.

CITIZEN. Some day, perhaps, he will be.

JUNIPER. Eh, man's world! how he loved it, and pitied it, and died for it! . . . Just like Christ, wasn't he?

CITIZEN. Almost.

JUNIPER. God forgive me! Often I found it hard to know the difference.

CITIZEN. God will show it you, Brother, some day.

JUNIPER. I'm afraid He will.

CITIZEN. Fear nothing that God does, Brother.

JUNIPER. You're right! Now you've told me something! Sure, 'twas love brought us to this meeting.

[*A crowd begins to appear in the gateway. Hands point. The crowd advances.*

135

CITIZEN. If so, then tell me who you are.

JUNIPER. Aye ; if you 'll not tell it to others. . . .
O Lord ! Somebody 's been and told 'em, and here
they 're all coming for me !

CITIZEN. Why so fearful, Brother—Juniper ?

JUNIPER. I, the greatest of sinners, and they
thinking me so holy !

[*He makes a bolt for the see-saw, turns off one of
the* Boys, *and mounts in his place.*

Here ! off with you ! Get to the other end ! Now
swing ! Up and away. And God save us all from
holiness !

CITIZEN [*laughing*]. Brother ! Brother !

JUNIPER [*as he swings*]. Aye, Brother, Brother !
And Brothers, all the rest of you ! And if it 's a
great sinner ye 're after, and want to know the like
of him—it 's me here ! Look !

[*The crowd, full of movement, excitement, and
curiosity, has now gathered round, and amid
a babble of contending voices the see-sawing
goes on—*JUNIPER *at the one end, the two* Boys
at the other.

CROWD [*confusedly, and together*]. Who is this fellow ? What mockery is here ? Where is the holy
man ? Where is Brother Juniper ? This fellow is
an impostor, a fool, a madman ! Seize him ! Stop
him ! Have him whipped ! Off with him !

CITIZEN [*mounting the pile*]. Listen, Brothers !

[*The uplifting of his hand imposes silence on the
crowd.* JUNIPER *stops swinging. He mounts
the plank, and stands balancing.*

JUNIPER. Aye ; ye 'd better, then. For if you
don't, destruction 's waiting for all of you, and the

Devil 's going to make his dinner off you, with me for a top-dressing. So now, then !

CITIZEN [*to the murmuring crowd*]. Listen ! Listen !

JUNIPER. There was a sinner once—as there always is—whose only use was to go about the world showing himself for what he was, that other sinners might take example by him, so as to be different. And sure, the mere sight of him so frightened 'em into their senses, that he did God's work—so far as their legs went, anyway—for they all ran away from him.

Now, that God should get such help from a sinner, pleased ill his lordship, the Devil. So one day he goes ahead to the place next on his way, and says to wise fools that were in it : ' There 's a holy man coming ! And, please God, ye 've all got to be like him.' So there was ruination waiting to fall on the whole city, and make 'em all sinners together of the worst kind ; and the Devil licking his lips ready for the taste of it—to have 'em all holy like him. But by God's mercy, from just round the corner, the sinner heard him saying it. ' Holy am I ? ' says he. ' And they 're to be like me, are they ? Is it holiness to lay eggs for Hell, and me be the hen hatching 'em ? O Lord, save 'em from me, and teach me what the Devil 's to be done now ! ' And the Lord said to that sinner, ' If ever there were two fools in this world, you 're one, and the Devil 's the other. Why, you 've only to be yourself, same as you always are, and they 'll catch fright at the mere sight of ye.' ' Holy ? ' He says. ' The Devil can't play the harps of Heaven by swiping 'em with his tail—much though he would like, maybe ! '

So the sinner went into the city with joy, and the

Lord saved it from him, showing him what a fool
he was for thinking any in their right senses would
mistake him for a holy man.

Look now, and you 'll all see it plain !

*[Suiting the action to the word, as he stands
centre, he sets the see-saw in motion, and times
his words to the rise and fall of it.*

For this was all that he had to tell :
You go up to Heaven, you go down to Hell ;
God 's above, the Devil 's below.
God 's for love, the Devil 's for woe ;
The deaf to God, to the Devil must hark ;
God 's the light, the Devil 's the dark ;
In the last and least God lights a spark,
On the back of a beast He makes His mark ;
The spirit of Love can ride on an ass,
And the Word of the Lord bring things to pass.
So Humpty Dumpty, hey diddle-dee !
That 's why the Spirit rides on me !

*[Suddenly a man of the crowd stands forward,
and points.*

MAN. That 's Brother Juniper !

JUNIPER. Aye ! Him that you thought holy.
And if the sight of him hasn't made you run away
from him yet, it 's time he ran away from you !

[Which accordingly he does.

CITIZEN. Well run, Brother Juniper.

CROWD. Brother Juniper !

*[The citizens stare in bewildered amazement, as
JUNIPER with his holiness becomes an in-
significant spot in the distance.*

CURTAIN

HOLY DISOBEDIENCE

In the corner of a small ante-chamber, past which runs a wide corridor, JUNIPER *has found a quiet hiding-place; and there sits nursing his fears. He is also nursing a pair of shoes, into the fastening-straps of which he has now driven the hole—finishing-touch to a work otherwise completed.* JUNIPER'S *fears are of the most depressing kind; weighed down and miserable, he sits hunched; then, at the sound of feet in the corridor, he starts with nervous apprehension. Brothers are passing—a crowd of them—for it is the whole community. Consistory is over. One—*BROTHER PACIFICO—*turns aside and enters; but does not perceive* JUNIPER *till he hears a voice.*

JUNIPER. What have they done to him, Brother?

PACIFICO [*in shocked surprise*]. You were not there, Brother?

JUNIPER [*dull of tone*]. No, Brother.

PACIFICO [*scenting an irregularity*]. Did you get leave from Father Minister Elias to stay away?

JUNIPER. No, Brother.

PACIFICO. Then you have broken discipline, Brother!

JUNIPER. Yes, Brother. . . . I 'll have to do penance for it.

PACIFICO. For such breach of discipline the penance is now a heavy one.

139

JUNIPER. Yes, Brother, I know that.

PACIFICO. Alas, I fear he will have you scourged for it.

JUNIPER. Not more than he's scourged Brother Leo for what *he* did.

PACIFICO. Aye; for he also has gone against the Rule, and broken discipline.

JUNIPER. Obeying the little Father.

PACIFICO. That was under the old Rule, Brother. Now the little Father is dead, we have not to observe it, having been given another.

JUNIPER. Aye; 'another' you can well call it! They'd scourge the little Father, if he were alive now!

PACIFICO [*horrified*]. Brother!

JUNIPER. Dead, and gone to glory! which now I've got to thank God for. What's Brother Leo done, but what we should all have done, had we been faithful to the little Father.

PACIFICO. We are under holy obedience to those in authority, Brother.

JUNIPER. Aye. But when you've two holy obediences pulling you two different ways, Brother, to two ends—what are ye to do then? Brother Leo gives holy obedience to the one, you give it to the other. It's either the little Father, and the Rule as he made it for us; or the Rule as it is now—made different.

PACIFICO. How different, Brother?

JUNIPER. The little Father said we were to have nothing of our own—ever.

PACIFICO. And still we have not.

JUNIPER. No. They've tied our legs with a lie; and we've let them.

PACIFICO. I fear, Brother, that I ought not even to listen to you.

JUNIPER. I 'm not asking ye to.

PACIFICO. We must not speak against those that are in authority, Brother.

JUNIPER. No; but, living or dead, we can mourn for 'em. And I 'll just tell you something I saw yesterday; you can give it what meaning you like. 'Twas a goat tied to a stake by a rope—giving her just so much run and no more. So long as she didn't pull, the rope lay loose; but when she pulled, the rope wasn't so long as she wanted it. Aye, and she could see the rope, Brother: but she couldn't see the stake it was tied to—for it being over the other side of a wall. Aye: couldn't see, so didn't know. But the stake had got her fast; and the rope was the authority which tied her to it. We still don't have anything of our own, you say? But there—round the corner, some one else has got it for us, and isn't going to give it away from us—not to any one, not if he came starving and begging, wanting it more than we did. Houses, land, money—all safely ours now—' for the glory of God ' they call it. But it 's not how the little Father meant it. And if he didn't mean it, God didn't mean it either.

PACIFICO. I fear that you are in sin, Brother.

JUNIPER. I 'm sure of it. Where 's Brother Leo?

PACIFICO. In the chapel, praying.

JUNIPER. Oh? So they let him do that.

PACIFICO. Father Minister gave him permission.

JUNIPER. Sure, man's mercies are wonderful! God's couldn't be better——

PACIFICO. Brother!

JUNIPER. —than some of 'em. So they let him pray ? And what are they going to do to him, when he 's done praying ?

PACIFICO. Because he would not submit himself to authority, he is to leave the Order.

JUNIPER. Leave the Order ? How can he ? The little Father brought him in ; and 'tisn't the little Father turns him out ; is it, Brother ?

PACIFICO. The little Father gave his authority to Ministers.

JUNIPER. And the Rule also. And 'twas for the care of the Rule they had authority. Only for that, Brother. But now they are breaking Brother Leo for keeping it. . . . When does he go ?

[*Three other* Brothers *have halted in passing and now stop to listen.*

PACIFICO. He goes now—if he has not gone already.

JUNIPER. Are we all going to see him off ?

PACIFICO. Nay, for none of us may speak to him.

JUNIPER [*muttering*]. Oh, I wasn't there. It 's an order I haven't heard.

PACIFICO. What did you say ?

JUNIPER. I was calling myself to obedience, Brother. Goes, does he ? Was it put to the vote ?

PACIFICO. No, Brother. Why should it be ?

JUNIPER. If we vote for a Brother to be Father Minister, oughtn't we to vote for a Brother not to be a Brother ?

PACIFICO. Having voted for one to have authority, Brother, he *has* the authority ; and we obey.

JUNIPER. I 've got to run a race for it, then !

[*He gets up and moves to go.*

PACIFICO. Where are you going, Brother ?

JUNIPER. To the chapel—to pray. Is that forbidden me ?

[*There is no answer, for at that moment* FATHER ELIAS *enters. Passing the other* Brothers, *with a quick gesture of dismissal which they obey, he comes to* JUNIPER.

ELIAS. Brother Juniper, where have you been ?

JUNIPER. Here, Father.

ELIAS. Were you not in the consistory with the rest ?

JUNIPER. No, Father.

ELIAS. Did you not *know* that you were to come ?

JUNIPER. Yes, Father.

ELIAS. What is your excuse ?

JUNIPER. None, Father.

[FATHER ELIAS *pauses for a moment. The defencelessness of* JUNIPER *puzzles him.*

ELIAS. *Why* did you not come ?

JUNIPER. I was disobedient, Father.

ELIAS. *Why* were you disobedient ?

[JUNIPER *has no wish for evasion, but it takes him a moment or two to get the thing said.*

JUNIPER. Because I hadn't a mind for what you were doing, Father.

ELIAS. How had you ' not a mind.'

JUNIPER. I felt it wasn't right, Father.

ELIAS. Whence got you that, Brother ?

JUNIPER. From the little Father. [*Then to himself.*] Ah, now I 've said it, and I 'm done for !

[*Here, then, in meeker form, is the rebellion of* BROTHER LEO *repeating itself.*

143

ELIAS. Brother Juniper, do you, also, seek to be cast out of the Order for disobedience to authority?

JUNIPER. No, Father.

ELIAS. But how can you hope to remain *in* the Order, Brother, if you refuse to obey?

JUNIPER. When I do not obey, Father, let me be punished for it, as I deserve.

[*Again the simplicity of* JUNIPER *gives pause to a mind too clever to understand him.*

ELIAS. Did you not *mean* to disobey?

JUNIPER. Yes, Father.

ELIAS. But now you say that you are willing to receive punishment?

JUNIPER. Yes, Father. If it be your will to punish me, I am willing, Father.

ELIAS. That is well said, Brother. But I find it hard to understand. Have you an equal will to disobey and to receive punishment?

JUNIPER. No, Father; I don't want to disobey— ever. I 'm sorry. It breaks my heart, Father.

ELIAS. That is well said, Brother. But you *have* disobeyed.

JUNIPER. Yes, Father.

ELIAS. Therefore must do penance.

JUNIPER. Yes, Father.

ELIAS. And the penance I shall now lay on you, you will perform, willingly—obediently?

JUNIPER. Yes, Father.

ELIAS. As due?

JUNIPER. Yes, Father.

ELIAS [*tortuously pursuing one who is too simple for him*]. For what?

JUNIPER. For setting myself against order and authority, Father.

ELIAS. For which you ask God to pardon you?

JUNIPER. Yes, Father; I ask God to pardon me for everything—every day, while He lets me live.

ELIAS. That is a good mind to be in, Brother. Hear, then, and obey! It is now near Angelus. As soon as the Angelus is over, you will go to the cell of correction, and there offer yourself for penance.

JUNIPER. Yes, Father.

ELIAS. Which Brother Jerome and Brother Simon will give you according to my instruction.

JUNIPER. Yes, Father.

ELIAS. And for any further breach of Rule or discipline into which you may fall, I now charge it to you on holy obedience that you come straightway and make confession, taking for it such penance as may be due.

JUNIPER. Yes, Father.

ELIAS. That is all, Brother. You may go.

[JUNIPER *starts to go, then kneels. And, as he does so, neither perceives, in the corridor without,* BROTHER LEO, *who, as he passes, halts sharply, and waits.*

JUNIPER. Father Minister, Brother Elias, pray for me!

ELIAS. I will, Brother.

JUNIPER. And for Brother Leo will you pray also, Father—that he may come back to us?

[*There is no answer,* FATHER ELIAS *turns abruptly away, and leaves* JUNIPER *kneeling. Slowly he rises, dry sobs catching his breath, and returns desolate to his seat. He takes up the*

*shoes he has laid down; and pressing his
hands over them finds in them a sort of comfort
and purpose in his desolation.* LEO *enters;
his face is a mask, covering the suffering he has
borne. He is not broken by it, but hardened.*

LEO. Brother Juniper, I was there. I heard
you. Why did you ask Father Elias to pray for
me?

JUNIPER. Surely, Brother, don't we all need praying for? And to have others praying for us, isn't
it good for *them*?

LEO. There are some I would rather did *not* pray
for me.

JUNIPER. Then God grant they do! For they're
the ones whose prayer you're most needing.
Wouldn't the little Father wish us to pray all for
all alike—richest and poorest? Aye, didn't he
himself, on his way to glory, ask sinners to pray for
him?—Sinners, Brother.

LEO. That was to help *them*, Brother.

JUNIPER. Aye: but it helped him too. Who did
he ever let go that prayed for him?

LEO. None, none! Oh, pray for *me*, Brother
Juniper!

JUNIPER. I do, Brother; I do it more for you
than for myself—just now.

LEO. Knowing what has been done to me?

JUNIPER. Yes, Brother.

LEO. Were you one of them—that consented?

JUNIPER. I wasn't there, Brother.

LEO. But you were *all* there.

JUNIPER. I wasn't, Brother.

LEO [*surprised*]. You were *not* there—with the rest!

JUNIPER. No: being disobedient. And now I 've to be sorry for it—which I am, Brother. And 'll have to be again ; for now 's the second time. But I 'd have been sorrier to be there. 'Twas a sorry choice, Brother ; but I made it. When there 's two sorrows in the way, and no getting past 'em, you have to choose one or other, like Our Lord did on the Cross, making His Mother's heart break for Him. We don't doubt He was sorry for it, Brother ; but He couldn't wish that sorrow away. 'Twas a *right* sorrow.   *[There is a pause.*

LEO [*greatly moved*]. Brother Juniper, oh, speak to me !

JUNIPER. I *am* speaking to you, Brother dear.

LEO. But more, more ! Oh, give me of the sweetness of your wisdom ! For *my* heart is bitter !

JUNIPER. Not your heart, Brother : only a taste it 's had, maybe, that 's hard to get rid of. *You* can't be bitter, Brother : you that the little Father loved best of us all, and the one, maybe, that still loves him best—for best understanding him.

LEO. I pray, I pray that it may so be !

JUNIPER. But you can't do that, Brother, with a bitter heart. Only by tenderness and forgiveness can you get near the little Father.

LEO [*kneeling and embracing him*]. Or being near *you*, Brother !

JUNIPER. Me, sinner that I am ! Don't trust yourself to me, Brother ! Eh, when you did *that*, there was I so afraid lest any should come in and find us ; and what they 'd think of it—though only the truth maybe ! The little Father wouldn't have been afraid of any one.

LEO. But you, Brother, though you have fear, do always as *he* would.

JUNIPER. When I remember, Brother. Aye, blessed be God, that gave me the mind to remember! Oh, Brother dear, life's hard for us now: but we've only to look back to find blessing. For wasn't life lovely that had the little Father in it? Was there ever an hour, or a minute—him there— that didn't leave blessing?

LEO. All gone now!

JUNIPER. No, Brother: his blessing stays—else he'd never have given it us. What's a blessing, Brother, if it wears out like an old coat? You cast that; but you never cast off his blessing, Brother— never!

LEO. Others have done so.

JUNIPER. Aye, they think to: some have, maybe. But *you* haven't, Brother; nor I, please God.

LEO. No, Brother: *you* have not.

JUNIPER. So there's the little Father's blessing still on us—you and me: he's not taken it away, Brother: for we've not tired of it, either of us, yet. Gone; but left his cloak, to keep us warm, Brother.

LEO [*rapt into vision*]. My Father, my Father! The chariot of Israel, and the horsemen thereof!

JUNIPER. Yes, Brother, only look high enough, and it's all there. But we're going on foot, aren't we?—for a long while yet; same as he did. And see, here's something I've made for you; for I knew, or guessed what they'd do to you, maybe. You've a long way to go before you get where the little Father's prayer shall bring you to rest. So I've made you these shoes, Brother—for remembrance. They 're not mine, they 're not yours; they 're the little Father's—and that just means everybody's. And you 're to have them, Brother, to give to the first beggar that asks—for a sign that you 're doing as the little Father wished you to do—having nothing your own. Put them on, Brother!

[*He kisses them as he hands them over; and* LEO *receiving, kisses them also.*

Aye, Amen, Amen! God give you peace, Brother.

LEO. Brother Juniper, had Father Minister ordered me to receive my penance at your hands, it would not have been bitter to me, but sweet.

JUNIPER. God o' mercy! I couldn't have done it, Brother.

LEO. But I have your own word for it, Brother. ' A right sorrow,' you said. A right sorrow for you; for me blessing.

JUNIPER. Sure, it would have broken my heart!

LEO. And healed mine! Three hundred stripes were laid on me for penance—and no love. And I went out seeking it. Darkness, bitterness, pain, anger. And when I stood up before all to be condemned, there was still no love in it. I am to leave the Order, because I will obey no Rule but the little Father's. And when I came forth from that condemnation, it seemed to me there was no love anywhere left.

JUNIPER. Listen, Brother. There 's *many* love you; but daren't say so. Oh, the poor sinners we are! You 're out of it now, Brother. You 'll be lonely, but you 'll be free. Aye, you 'll starve, you 'll be cold, you 'll wander without a home; and you 'll hear men often reproach you. But the little Father—*he* knows. And here's the wonder of wonders—that I know the same as *he* knows. And there's only one thing that makes me know it —me, the fool I am—because out of him I learned how to love, Brother.

> [*The Angelus bell begins ringing.*

Now, after this, Brother, not a word!

Nunc dimittis, Domine!

LEO. Pax vobiscum.

> [*Together they kneel, crossing themselves, and together say the ' Ave.'*

Ave Maria gratiae plena, Dominus tecum. Benedicta tu in mulieribus; et benedictus fructus ventri tui, Jesu, Sancta Maria, Mater Dei, ora pro nobis pecatoribus, nunc et in hora mortis nostrae. Amen.

> [*They rise, look at each other, and part.* JUNIPER *watches* LEO *go. Along the corridor come* BROTHER JEROME *and* BROTHER SIMON, *each bearing a scourge. They look in and see* JUNIPER. SIMON *halts and makes a gesture. They are ready for the business. Angelus is over.*

JUNIPER. Yes, Brother, I'm coming.

> [*And with meek willingness he goes after them.*

CURTAIN

WEAKER VESSELS

To the gate of St. Damien's come two Brothers *of the* Friars Minor. *BROTHER ILLUMINATO *enters first, followed by* BROTHER JUNIPER. *They ring : and presently to the grille comes a* LAY SISTER.

ILLUMINATO. Is Reverend Mother in, Sister ?

LAY SISTER. She is never out, Brother.

ILLUMINATO. Will she see us, I mean : we being told we were not to come in here any more.

LAY SISTER. *She* did not say so, Brother.

ILLUMINATO. No : but 'twas said *for* her—by those we must obey.

LAY SISTER. I will call her, Brothers. [*She goes.*

JUNIPER. Ah ! 'Twasn't like this when we'd the Little Father with us. We were let come in freely then—sit, talk, and pray with them, like one of themselves.

ILLUMINATO. Does it matter, Brother ? So long as we may still see them. This gate does not prevent.

JUNIPER. But it means they are afraid of us.

CLARE [*appearing at the gate*]. They ? Who, Brother ?

JUNIPER [*turning*]. Ah, Sister dear, 'twasn't *you* I was meaning. If *you* didn't want us, you'd tell us straight, wouldn't you ?

CLARE. Yes, Brother. [*Then, to the* Lay Sister] Open the gate, Sister !

[*The* Lay Sister *opens it ;* CLARE *comes out.* As you may not come in to us, we must come out to you. . . . Bring a bench, Sister, and tell the others to come—all of them.

ILLUMINATO. Why mayn't we come in now, Sister ?

CLARE. The Holy Father thinks it is not good for us.

JUNIPER. That's the new Holy Father, isn't it, Sister ?

CLARE. Yes, Brother.

JUNIPER. The last Holy Father knew ; and *he* didn't mind. Why should this one ?

CLARE. Because, Brother, all minds not being alike, men often think differently.

ILLUMINATO. What are you going to do about it, Sister ?

CLARE. Teach the Holy Father to think better, Brother—you helping us.

JUNIPER. Teach ! *We* teach the Holy Father, Sister ?

CLARE. Why not ? Cannot the wise learn of the simple ?

JUNIPER. But were we to teach him as he did

not wish to be taught—wouldn't it be heresy, Sister ?

CLARE. No, Brother.

[*The* Lay Sister *has now returned, carrying the bench. The other* Sisters *follow her.*

Put open the gate, Sister : set the bench ; and all of you sit down, inside. That has not been forbidden to us—yet.

[*The bench is set inside the gateway ; the elders seat themselves, the younger stand behind. All the* Sisters, *and* CLARE *also, are thin and pale—for a reason that will presently be told.*

ILLUMINATO. How did you get word of it, Sister ?

CLARE. The Bishop himself came from Perugia with the Holy Father's blessing, and told us it was his wish.

JUNIPER. But why, Sister ?

CLARE. For fear lest it might cause scandal.

JUNIPER. Scandal ? And we Brothers and Sisters of the Little Father, now gone to his glory ! God forgive any that can think such a thing !

CLARE. Amen, Brother.

[*At the word ' scandal,' the* Sisters, *who have brought with them the mendings and darnings which they do for their Brothers of the Order, let go their needlework, and lifting hands and eyebrows of astonishment, indulge in that weakness of the herd-instinct, which the pious so easily fall into—the luxury of being ' shocked ' in a good cause.*

CLARE [*catching sight of them*]. Don't be foolish, Sisters—making faces like that! Go on with your work, and be useful!

SISTER ANGELA. Dear Reverend Mother, you told us to come and listen!

CLARE. Yes, Sister. But I did not tell you to come and look like fools.

JUNIPER. You mustn't look like me, Sisters.

CLARE. They didn't, Brother. I wish they did —sometimes.

JUNIPER. God forbid!

CLARE. He has, Brother.

ILLUMINATO [*waiting for the story to finish*]. Well, Sister?

CLARE. Well, Brother; that's all.

ILLUMINATO. But what have you done about it, so as to make the Holy Father (as you say) think better of it?

CLARE. I have sent word to the Holy Father that we will do as he tells us, till we hear from him again.

ILLUMINATO. And you have not heard from him?

CLARE. Not yet, Brother. For that was only three days ago; and though the Bishop went in great haste to tell him, he has hardly had time yet to bring back an answer.

ILLUMINATO. In great haste: why, Sister?

CLARE. Because, Brother, I told the Bishop something which the Holy Father had not thought about.

ILLUMINATO. What was it, Sister?

CLARE. Maybe I shall not have to tell you,

Brother, if the Holy Father, when he hears, thinks better of it.

JUNIPER. The Holy Father's got a lot to think about just now, Sister.

CLARE. He always has, Brother.

JUNIPER. Yes, Sister. But haven't you heard how he and the Emperor are having a pulling match together—which of them in this world's to be the biggest and the strongest, and have everyone to obey him?

CLARE. No, Brother; in here we have heard nothing. Obey? In what? How?

JUNIPER. It's like this, Sister: the Holy Father says that the Emperor must obey him in all things—always, and without question.

CLARE. Yes, Brother?

JUNIPER. But the Emperor says *not* in all things: only in things concerning the Faith. And *he* says, there are *some* things where the Holy Father has got to obey *him*.

[*This is a shock to some of the* Sisters: *but not to* CLARE.

CLARE. In what must the Holy Father obey *him*, Brother?

JUNIPER. In things that are of this world, he says; and that he has got Our Lord's own word for it . . . 'Render to Caesar,' he says, 'the things that are Caesar's.' And it's not to be denied that Our Lord did say so; didn't He, Sister?

CLARE. Yes, Brother. And what does the Holy Father say to that?

ILLUMINATO. He says that as everything belongs to God—or ought to—Caesar belongs to Him too.

And as he is the Voice of God here on earth, the Emperor must obey *him* in all things.

             [*Some of the* Sisters *very much agree.*

JUNIPER. And that's right, isn't it, Sister?

CLARE [*after a pause*]. I don't know, Brother. In matters of Faith, yes. But if the Holy Father told *me* to do something I knew to be wrong, *I* would not obey him.

ILLUMINATO. But can the Holy Father ever be wrong in what he tells us to do, Sister?

CLARE. Of course, Brother; for did not Blessed St. Paul himself tell Blessed St. Peter *he* was wrong, when he *was* wrong? And if St. Peter could make mistakes, so also can the Holy Father.

ILLUMINATO [*astonished*]. Then where *are* we, Sister?

CLARE. In the world, Brother; but in God's Hands also. What Holy Mother Church teaches —that is true; and we must believe it. But what those holding power and authority do, and would have others do, is not always the teaching of Holy Mother Church.

ILLUMINATO. But the Emperor, they say, is a foul liver; an infidel and an unbeliever.

CLARE. Yes, Brother; and therefore the more likely to be wrong, also, in what he does, and would have others do. But the Holy Father, though true in the Faith, and meaning well, may be wrong also.

ILLUMINATO. But are we to judge, Sister?

CLARE. No, Brother; we must leave it in God's Hands to decide: the matter being too great for our understanding.

ILLUMINATO. Then which of them are we to obey, Sister ?

CLARE. Our obedience, Brother, is to the Rule given us by the Little Father, while he was yet living. And that now having been confirmed to us by Holy Mother Church, it is ours for ever ; and we safe, if we abide by it.

ILLUMINATO. The Emperor gives no heed to what the Church says, Sister. Because the Holy Father has excommunicated him, he has brought over an army of Saracens to fight for him against the Holy Father ; since, he being under ex-communication, Christians dare not.

CLARE. But the Holy Father is not going to fight, is he, Brother ?

ILLUMINATO. Yes, Sister ; or has told others to do so for him. And some will ; but there's more that will not, being afraid of the Emperor—he being so mighty, strong, and terrible. So here's all Christendom divided, Sister. And (nobody knowing which side is going to win) there's no safety for any of us.

CLARE. But *why* are they fighting, Brother ? What is their quarrel ? What is it which, bidden by the Holy Father, the Emperor will not do ?

ILLUMINATO. He won't go to the Crusades, Sister, but in his own time, and in his own way, he says.

CLARE. What way is that, Brother ?

ILLUMINATO. He says that going to war—not having anything to do with the Faith—is for him and not for the Holy Father to decide. Matters of Faith, he says, belong to the Holy Father ; but law, order, and government to him. And he says that if the Holy Father decrees that there be five Persons to the Blessed Trinity instead of three, he'll believe it—or say so at any rate—and'll make others do the same. But peace and war, he says, are things of *this* world ; so he'll go on the Crusades only when it suits him to go ; and not when the Holy Father tells him. And the vow he took that he would go—which the Pope made him take, while still a child—was taken, he says, without choice or reason being given him ; so now he is not bound by it ; and he'll not go till he's done other things first, which more need doing. . . . Now, is that right, Sister ?

CLARE. I don't know, Brother. How can I know ?

ILLUMINATO. Then, when war comes, what are we to do about it ?

CLARE. We shall not fight, Brother. Our blessed Father, St. Francis, forbade fighting.

ILLUMINATO. But if the Holy Father tells people to fight for him, what else can they do— *but* fight ?

CLARE. Brother, at what time, think you, did the Passion of Our Lord begin ? Was it on the Cross only, when He gave Himself up to be slain ?

ILLUMINATO. Surely, Sister, in the Garden of Gethsemane, when, after He had prayed with the bloody sweat, the Betrayer came and kissed Him.

CLARE. No, Brother—not then ; for already had His other Disciples betrayed Him ; no longer believing His word.

JUNIPER. How, Sister ?

CLARE. Do you not remember, Brothers, how,

in the Upper Chamber, He asked them—' When I sent you forth without scrip, or purse, or shoes, lacked you anything ? ' And they said, ' Nothing.' What said He then ?—' Let him that hath a purse now take it, likewise his scrip ; and let him that hath no sword sell his garment and buy one.' . . . Why did He say that ?

JUNIPER. I don't know, Sister.

CLARE. Because, Brothers, it was their own way they were choosing then, not *His*. And He—reading their hearts—*knew*. While they went His way, they needed *no* swords ; but going their own way—the world's way—they would need them. And see, Brother, in that way they had already gone, secretly—not telling Him. For then one said, ' Here are two swords.' And He said, ' It is enough ! ' Surely, at that moment began the Passion of Our Lord, when—seeing they had already armed themselves—He knew that they no longer followed or trusted Him.

ILLUMINATO. But did He not tell them, Sister, that they *should* have swords ?

CLARE. Aye ; if they believed not in Him. But when, a short while after, Peter *used* his sword—what said He then ? ' Put up thy sword again into its place ; for they that take the sword shall perish with the sword.' And that which He spake then is truth for all time, to those who truly believe in Him. So, Brothers, if the Holy Father now takes the sword, shall *he* be right, when St. Peter himself was wrong ?

JUNIPER. You frighten me, Sister !

CLARE. Aye, Brother ? But if, obedient to

Christ and the Little Father, ye take not the sword, neither shall *ye* have fear. Did not our Little Father himself go and stand before the Soldan unarmed, and thence come forth free and without hurt ? Seem we in more peril now than he seemed then ? Yet what would the Soldan have done, had he slain him, but given him up into the glory wherein now he dwells ? And has not God as great a care for the Holy Father and for Holy Mother Church as He had then for him ?

THE BROTHERS. Surely, Sister.

CLARE. Aye, surely. So, if this Emperor, who obeys not his word, is an infidel, and strong, making men fear him—what matters it, if the Holy Father himself is a believer ? Pray, Brothers, that the Holy Father may have light and truth, and stand swordless without fear. Then will Holy Mother Church in his keeping be safe.

JUNIPER. Will you go and tell that to the Holy Father, Sister ?

CLARE. God will tell him in His own way, Brother. I may not go to the Holy Father unless he sends for me.   [*There is a pause.*

JUNIPER. Sister dear ; here's something we've come to ask you. And now's the time for it. . . . Are you angry with us, Sister ?

CLARE. I angry ? No, Brother.

JUNIPER. Nor grieved, Sister ?

CLARE. No, Brother.

JUNIPER. And you're not disappointed in us, Sister, for anything we've done, or not done, maybe ?

CLARE. No, Brother. Why ?

JUNIPER. And you are still glad to see us, Sister ?

CLARE. Yes, Brother, and shall be always.

JUNIPER. Well, Sister, we just wanted to know; because here's Brother Simon coming with the food we've got for you.

CLARE. God bless and reward your charity, Brothers. But to-day we have no use for it.

JUNIPER. Oh, not again, Sister !

                    [*Enter* SIMON *with basket.*

CLARE. Find others, Brother, who need it more than we do.

ILLUMINATO. Find others ? But why, Sister ? Have we not always brought food for you ?

CLARE. Yes, Brother.

ILLUMINATO. Then why not still ?

CLARE. Because, Brother, as the Holy Father has said that we may no longer receive from you food for our souls, lest it should cause scandal, neither will we receive food for our bodies !

JUNIPER. Sister ! Oh, Sisters ! Was that why you sent back what came yesterday—saying you had no use for it ?

CLARE. Yes, Brother.

THE SISTERS [*tremulously : some of them near to tears*]. Yes, yes, Brother.

JUNIPER. And the day before also ?

CLARE. Yes, Brother.

THE SISTERS [*some now dissolving into tears*]. Yes, yes, Brother !

JUNIPER [*aghast*]. Then you've had nothing to taste for three days, Sister ?

CLARE. No, Brother.

JUNIPER. Virgins and Martyrs! And what do all the others say to it?

SISTER URSULA [*weeping*]. That we are very hungry, Brother.

JUNIPER. Hungry! You must be dying!

CLARE. Not yet, Brother.

JUNIPER. Sister dear, is this right of you?

CLARE. Yes, Brother.

THE SISTERS [*tearfully*]. Yes, Brother.

SISTER ANNA. For what Reverend Mother wishes, we wish also. But, Brother dear [*to* SIMON], please take back the basket, or put it where we cannot see it. For that, indeed, is a sore trial to us—we knowing what is in it.

BROTHER SIMON. But ye *don't*, Sisters! For here's a roast goose, given to us by the Podesta, the better to tempt you; he hearing that these last two days you'd lost your appetites. But whether it's you, or the Holy Father himself, who ought now to be eating it, Heaven alone knows and can say, for I cannot!

SISTER URSULA. Roast goose! I smell it! Oh, Brother, in quick mercy and for kind charity take it away! Reverend Mother, tell him to take it away!

THE SISTERS. Yes, yes, Mother, let him take it away!

[*While the* Sisters *are thus lamentably fighting against temptation, a* Messenger *enters, and stands looking on in stately amazement, till* CLARE *lifts up her hand and commands silence.*

MESSENGER. Reverend Mother, I come from my Lord, the Bishop, returned this very hour from

Perugia, bringing for you a message from the Holy
Father.

> [CLARE *and all the* Sisters *assume an attitude
> of submissive reverence, standing with hands
> crossed and heads bent.*

The Holy Father sends you his blessing, and says
that, on holy obedience, you are not to starve
yourselves—neither in the things of this world,
nor in the things of the next. And the Holy
Father says further, that if, searching your con-
science truly, you find the ministry of your little
Brothers of the Friars Minor helpful to your Community, in things pertaining to salvation, then
they may come in and go out, and be with you
as aforetime—but only at certain hours, namely
from one hour after dawn till one hour before sunset—not earlier and not later, so as not to cause
offence to weaker vessels. Reverend Mother,
I have given you the Holy Father's message,
as by my Lord, the Bishop, it was given to
me. In nomine Patris, et Filii, et Spiritus Sancti.
Amen.

> [*He turns and goes without waiting for an
> answer.*

CLARE. Oh, Brothers, now God has rewarded your
charity, and has won for it the Holy Father's
blessing. Bring in the basket, Brother.

SIMON. No, Sister ; for look, it is already sunset
and past the hour which the Holy Father has ruled
for us.

CLARE. Very well, Brother, leave it.

JUNIPER [*snatching up the basket and handing
it*]. Go in, go in, Sister Goose, where we may

not ! And may she be the saving of you, Sisters ! Though—being but one among so many, she'll not go far, I'm thinking.

> [*The basket has been caught by a dozen out-stretched hands: for* Sister Goose *is indeed very welcome.*

CLARE. Enough for to-day, Brothers. To-morrow come again.

JUNIPER. Oh, Sister dear, had she known that she was going to be the life and the saving of you, how she must have praised God for it ! And could any goose have wished for a better death ?

CLARE. Perhaps not, Brother.

JUNIPER. *I* couldn't ! Please God, and the Little Father, make *my* end to be like hers ! Amen !

CURTAIN

HOLY TERROR

*Between the Convent build-
ings of St. Damien's is a
narrow terrace ; and at the
far end of it, a strip of
garden raised a few feet
above the rest. This terrace
overlooks the Convent garden
which lies outside the walls
below. Two steps lead up
to the raised garden from the
terrace. One of the* Sisters—
Angela—*is filling a few pots
with soil. The Angelus rings ; she stops, crosses herself, and
mutters the 'Ave Maria.' She has just resumed her work when,
from a side-door, two of the* Sisters *enter, carrying* Reverend
Mother Clare *in a sort of chair-litter, with side-handles for
carrying it by. They set her down close to her garden.*

CLARE. Are you ready for me, Sister ?

ANGELA. Yes, Reverend Mother ; here are four
pots waiting ; and I am filling two others.

CLARE. Bring me one ; and the seedlings.

[*A pot is brought, and a low bowl set thick with
seedlings. These* CLARE *begins to transplant.
She handles them like a born gardener.*

CLARE. Yes, Sisters, you can leave me. I need
only Sister Angela to help me now. [*They go.*]
Sister Angela, get some water.

[ANGELA *goes out to the right; from the other end a* Sister *enters.*

SISTER. Reverend Mother ; a messenger.

CLARE. Where from, Sister ?

SISTER. From Assisi.

CLARE. Who sends him ?

SISTER. Father Minister Elias, Mother. 'Tis Brother Jerome. He says it is very urgent.

CLARE. Ask him to come here into the garden, Sister. Say I am sorry my feet will not let me come down to-day. But I can speak to him from here.

[*The* Sister *goes.* SISTER ANGELA *has now returned with the water. From a distance comes a sudden clanging of bells.* SISTER ANGELA *starts and stumbles.*

CLARE. What are all those bells ringing for ?

ANGELA. Alas ! Reverend Mother, that is the warning that we have been expecting, telling the country-folk to come into the city to be safe.

CLARE. Are you sure, Sister ? How do you know ?

ANGELA. Years ago, Little Mother, I heard the same, when we were at war with Perugia.

CLARE. ' We,' Sister ?

ANGELA. The citizens of Assisi, Mother ; and I myself was then living down there in the valley outside. We had all to run to the city for our lives, as fast as we could go. I was a child, but I remember it well : the very sound of it still frightens me.

CLARE. Why should the *sound* frighten you,

Sister ? 'Tis only four bells, all tolling together. Would three frighten you less, and five frighten you more ?

ANGELA. I am frightened at what it means, Reverend Mother.

CLARE. 'Twill be time enough to be frightened, if you must be frightened, when its meaning comes. Till then——

ANGELA [*looking*]. Reverend Mother, Brother Jerome is there below—waiting.

CLARE. Help me, Sister.

[*Assisted, she rises from her chair and looks over into the garden below.*

Ah ! Brother Jerome, welcome ! God be with you ! You bring a message from Father Minister, they tell me.

JEROME [*from below*]. Yes, Reverend Mother. Father Elias sent me in haste. 'Tis very urgent : but I was to give it to you alone.

CLARE. Come up the steps, Brother ; then you will be nearer. I cannot stand long.

JEROME. I do not see any steps, Reverend Mother.

CLARE. We call them steps, Brother. Those holes in the wall. It is the short way by which some of the Sisters go down into the garden and come up again.

JEROME. Can I climb those, Reverend Mother ?

CLARE. God helping you, yes, Brother. . . . Sister Angela, let down the rope !

[ANGELA *throws down a rope, the upper end of which is fastened to a beam in the wall.*

There, also, is a rope to help you, Brother. Now

go, Sister : and tell the others that no one else is to come till I call.

> [ANGELA *goes, just as* BROTHER JEROME'S *head appears over the wall. He throws his arms over the parapet, and so keeps himself in position for the talk that follows.* CLARE *has again seated herself.*

CLARE. Well, Brother ?

JEROME. Reverend Mother, Father Elias sends word that to-day there is like to be danger ; but that afterwards—if that which he has put in hand prospers—all will again be safe.

CLARE. What is the danger, Brother ?

JEROME. The Saracen troops which the Emperor has brought from overseas to fight for him in his War against the Holy Father are coming this way to-day in their march upon Perugia. And 'tis said that, when they have taken Perugia, they will come back and take Assisi also, if the gates be not already open to them. So Father Elias has sent messengers to the Emperor, praying him to take the Order into his favour and protection. And when the Emperor has granted that prayer— which surely he will grant—then all we in the Order, the Sisters as well as the Brothers, will be safe—no matter what happens, either here or in Perugia.

CLARE. Safe from what, Brother ?

JEROME. From the army of the Saracens, Reverend Mother, that are in the Emperor's service.

CLARE. Fighting against our Holy Father, the Pope, Brother ?

JEROME. Yes, Reverend Mother; for that we cannot help—nor do we approve of it.

CLARE. Then wherefore does Father Minister Elias ask his protection?

JEROME. Because, being followers of our Blessed Father St. Francis, now with God, we have nothing to do with wars, nor can we take part in them. So, being at peace with all, may we not seek protection of all? And though the Emperor have sinned grievously against the Holy Father, and Holy Mother Church, this is no sin that Father Minister would have him do, but contrary rather; so that for all his wrong-doing he may yet do one thing that, in some measure, may hereafter win for him mercy and forgiveness.

CLARE. The protection of such as he, Brother, I seek not; nor can I trust it, if it be offered. Is not God's protection enough for us, if we have faith for it?

JEROME. Not in this world, Reverend Mother; not always—not to-day. Therefore to-day—with danger so near to us—Father Elias sends word for you and all the Sisters to come at once into the city, where lodging shall be found for you till danger be over.

CLARE. Tell Father Minister that we thank him for the care and thought he had for us. But I think not that any will come.

JEROME. Not come, Reverend Mother? Hast a mind for what would happen, were the Infidel to come and find any of the Sisters still here?

CLARE. Aye, Brother. But we have here some that are sick and cannot be moved. We cannot leave them—*I* cannot. But if any of the Sisters wish to go—they shall go.

JEROME. How many, think you, Reverend Mother? I ask, so that lodging may be found for them.

CLARE. I think—none, Brother. But, if any, I will shortly send word after you.

JEROME. Alas, I fear that Father Minister will judge me to have been a poor pleader for that he would see done.

CLARE. Tell Father Minister from me, Brother, that you have delivered your message well ; and that you are not to blame ; for that, had he come himself, I should have given him the same answer.

JEROME. Well, Reverend Mother, I *have* delivered it : so there is no more to say. But have a mind —should you change it—how short now is the time. For we heard that ere noon the Saracens were already on the road this side Foligno, and coming on fast, they said.

CLARE. Well, Brother, the sooner they be here, the sooner they will be gone. Farewell ! Hold fast by the rope, and see that you fall not. . . . [JEROME *disappears.*] . . . Safe ?

JEROME [*from below*]. Aye : safe so far, Reverend Mother ; but in the city I shall be safer.

> [CLARE *takes up the flower-pot again, and is about to resume her gardening when* SISTER ZAREPHA *puts in a disobedient head—other heads showing behind her, and almost at once other voices joining in her petition.*

ZAREPHA. Oh, Reverend Mother, let me come in ! I *must* come in ! Do not forbid us to come in,

Reverend Mother! We are here all of us! Grant us, on holy obedience, that we may come in.

THE SISTERS. Yes: Reverend Mother, let us come in!

CLARE. Come in, Sisters! Come all of you.

MONICA. Reverend Mother! Have you heard the news?

CLARE. If it be the same news that Brother Jerome has just brought me, I have heard it, Sister.

URSULA. The army of the Infidels is coming, Little Mother.

CLARE. Yes; that is what he told me.

ANNA. Coming *here*, Mother! Coming *here*! Oh, if they come, what shall we do?

CLARE. Brother Jerome brought word from Father Minister Elias, that, if we wished, we might go into the city, and that there he would find lodging for us.

MONICA. Then, Little Mother, let us go quickly: for word has come that the Saracens are approaching. Some say that, from the walls of the city, they have already seen them.

CLARE. Any of you that wish may go, Sisters. But I shall not go. Also there are some of us sick that cannot.

URSULA. But those that are sick we can carry, Little Mother.

CLARE. Not all of them, Sister; and even if all the rest could go, I should stay here.

ZAREPHA. You would not go, Mother?

CLARE. No, Sister.

ZAREPHA. Why not, Mother?

CLARE. Because in Assisi I should not feel any safer than I feel here. But if any of you believe that you *will* be safer in Assisi, you may go and leave me. There is nothing in the Rule against it, if it be found necessary for the saving of life.

MONICA. But we cannot go without *you*, Little Mother.

CLARE. Why not, Sister ?

MONICA. Surely, Mother, you *know* that we cannot.

CLARE. How do I know it, Sister ?

MONICA. Because you know how we love and trust you. And without you, nowhere should we feel safe.

CLARE. But surely, Sister, you love and trust God more than you do me : so in His Hands must feel far safer than in mine.

URSULA. Yes, Little Mother, if we knew that it was His will for us to stay here, then maybe we should be able so to believe and feel.

CLARE. But do you not believe that it was God's will that I should be your Little Mother, and have the care and keeping of you ?

MONICA. None of us can doubt *that*, Mother dear.

CLARE. Then doubt nothing, Sisters ; for if I had any doubt I would bid you go. But if you have none—then stay.

> [*Meanwhile, in the distance, there has been a confused murmur of sound which now grows louder, though still some distance away. A far-off blast of trumpets is heard.*

ANNA. Oh, hark, what is that ?

CLARE. Trumpets, Sister. Have you never heard trumpets before?

[SISTER ANNA *goes up to the rampart.*

ANNA. Oh, look, look, look!

[*The* Sisters *all crowd to look, with exclamations of fear in various degrees.*

CLARE [*who remains seated*]. What is it you see, Sisters?

URSULA. It is the army of the Saracens. They are here already.

CLARE. Not *here*, Sister.

URSULA. But they are coming, Mother; *some* of them are coming. Look, a great troop of them is coming along the road just below.

ANNA. Oh, Little Mother, why were you so sure? It is too late now! Too late for any of us. Oh, if it were not too late, I think that some of us would wish to go now.

CLARE. Where are the Lay Sisters? Go, one of you, and call them in. They should be in here with all the rest of us.

MONICA. I think they have gone, Mother; to the city.

CLARE. But they did not come and ask me if they might go.

ZAREPHA. Little Mother, they are here, they are here!

[*The four* Lay Sisters *enter.*

CLARE. Ah, that is well! Come in, Sisters. But which of you is it that to-day should have rung the bell for nones? [*One of the* Sisters *indicates herself.*] You are late, Sister. Go.

SOME OF THE SISTERS. Oh, Reverend Mother,

don't ring the bell! If you ring the bell, they will hear us.

CLARE. Why should they not hear us? They have seen us already.

ANGELA. Aye, look, Mother, look! They are making signals. Hark! An order has been given.

THE SISTERS. Oh, Little Mother, save us!

[*At that moment the Chapel-bell begins tolling.*

CLARE. Say your office here, Sisters, to-day, and begin at once.

ZAREPHA. How can we say our office here, Mother, with danger so near at hand?

CLARE. All the better, Sister. For if you think you are in danger, saying your office will be better help than crying about it. Come quickly, two of you, and help me to the Chapel. The rest of you, on holy obedience, stay here.

THE SISTERS [*speaking all together in different sentences*]. Little Mother, where are you going?

Ah! Little Mother, don't leave us!

Oh, Little Mother, don't go! don't go! Come back!

[*Then the last one, alone:*

Why are you going, Little Mother?

CLARE. To bring Our Blessed Lord to help and protect us.

ANNA. Nothing can help us now. Nothing can save us! [*She grovels.*]

[*Supported by two of the* Sisters, CLARE *goes haltingly out.*

THE SISTERS [*dispersedly*]. Ah! look, look! They are coming this way! Yes; the main troop is marching along the valley; but a body of them

174

has turned and is coming here! Twenty, thirty, forty, fifty: I count fifty of them! They see us: they are pointing!

[*A shout comes from a distance and is repeated in a tone of savage jeering exultation.*

They are running! Oh, God of Mercy! God of Mercy! Pity us! Protect us! Save us!

[*The* Sisters *run here and there in wild panic, catching at each other, and breaking away again.*

THE SISTERS [*dispersedly*]. The Little Mother told us to stay!

Oh, why did she tell us to stay?

Oh, why on holy obedience must I stay to be defiled and slain by the Infidels?

Little Mother! Little Mother!

[*One of the* Sisters *mounts the step to the terraced garden, and looks over, and down. With a loud scream, she rushes away toward the door into the Convent. The head of a Saracen appears over the wall; then another. They mount; others come pressing after them. The* Sisters *all rush, wailing and screaming, toward the door. Through the door comes* CLARE, *walking erect and unassisted, but with great pain and feebleness. After her come the two* Sisters, *trembling and crouching with fear.* CLARE *carries the Monstrance, containing the Blessed Sacrament, raised high in her hands. Some of the Saracens are now on the top of the rampart, trampling down the flowers of* CLARE'S *garden. As she enters, two of them leap down on to the terrace and are about to advance.* CLARE, *through the frightened crowd of crouching and clinging* Sisters, *moves calmly toward them.*

CLARE. In nomine Patris, et Filii, et Spiritus Sancti. [*With the Monstrance she makes the sign of the Cross.*]

> [*A silence gradually falls among the wailing* Sisters : *they turn and gaze in wonder, as* CLARE *slowly advances alone upon the Saracens, bearing the Host before her, the shouting of the Saracens changing to a note of mingled rage and fear. As she advances they retreat before her. Meanwhile* CLARE *continues to pray swiftly, in a voice of serene confidence :*

Salvos fac servos tuos, Deus meus, sperantes in te. Mitte eis, Domine, auxilium in sancto. Domine, exaudi orationem meam ; et clamor meus ad te veniet.

> [*The Saracens have not waited ; backing confusedly as she advances, stumbling, beating each other to make way, they remount the terrace rampart, tumble across it, and disappear. Mounting slowly after them,* CLARE *bestows on them a final elevation of the Host for their blessed discomfiture. Then, turning on the step to the kneeling* Sisters, *who are now gazing at her in tearful adoration, she recites the Gloria :*

Gloria Patri, et Filio, et Spiritui Sancto, Sicut erat in principio, et nunc, et semper, et in saecula saeculorum. Amen. Alleluia.

> [*On the last word she sways with weakness, and seems about to fall. Two of the* Sisters *start*

*up and run to her aid. With difficulty she
descends the steps, still bearing the Monstrance
before her.*

Sisters, help me, and uphold me, while I bear
the Blessed Sacrament back to the Altar.

*[Supported by the two Sisters, she advances
slowly : every movement shows the exhaustion
that has now come upon her. Suddenly she
stops, and sways backward : raising the Host
high as she sinks back into the supporting
arms, she cries to another of the Sisters :*

Take ! Sister. Take !

*[The Sister, springing forward, receives the Mon-
strance from her.* CLARE *falls back in a dead
faint.*

THE SISTERS. Little Mother ! Little Mother !
Little Mother !

CURTAIN

LOVERS MEETING

(1240)

It is winter. The Community-house of the Friars Minor in Perugia lies open toward the street, through a doorway of roughly hewn timber. Exterior steps lead down; interior steps lead up to the workshops and cells of the community. In a corner of one of these BROTHER GILES *sits across a bench, very busy at shoe-mending. As he works, he sings; his hammer beating time to the music. In the pause of his song, one hears in the distance a tucket of trumpets blown, to which he pays no heed.*

GILES [*singing*].
 ' Who knocks to-night so late? '
  The weary porter said.
 Three kings stood at the gate;
  Each with a crown on head.

 The serving-man bowed down;
  The inn was full, he knew.
 Said he, ' In all this town
  Is no fit place for you.'

[*While he sings,* BROTHER RUFUS *enters from the street, laden with vegetables.*

179

A light the manger lit ;
   There lay the Mother meek.
   Said they ' This place is fit——'

                  [Trumpets sound again.

RUFUS. What makes you so busy, Brother ?

GILES [*hammering as he sings*]. ' Here is the rest
we seek.'

RUFUS. Eh ? Can you not answer ?

GILES. Brother Juniper left me these shoes to
mend ; and I a poor hand at it.

RUFUS. Ah ? I saw him down by the walls just
now, along with the beggars. There was a great
crowd looking over.

GILES. What to see ?

RUFUS. Along the valley troops marching.

GILES [*stopping his work*]. Is there another war—
already ?

RUFUS. No : only the old one. Crusaders from
France and Milan, so I was told. In the gate there
were five knights on horseback—one talking to the
Podesta.

GILES. Are they coming here ?

RUFUS. Why, no : there are thousands. We
shouldn't have room. But they have buyers all
about the market, wanting horses. One of them
spoke to me.

GILES. Had you a horse to sell, Brother ?

RUFUS. *He* wasn't wanting a horse. He was
asking me (seeing I was one of them) where the
Brothers lived ; and whether——

   [*Enter an* OLD BEGGAR *trailing a piece of cloth.*

BEGGAR. What 's the use ? Fool ! He 's only

given me half !   What 's the use of half ?   It won't
cover my legs.

GILES. God give you patience, Brother.   What 's
the matter ?

BEGGAR. Matter ?   To this there 's not matter
enough !   That 's what 's the matter.

[GILES, *leaving his work, comes down, takes hold
of the cloth, and examines it.*   RUFUS *takes in
the vegetables, then returns and begins to draw
water from a fountain set in the wall.*

BEGGAR [*peevishly snatching back the cloth*]. Who
are you ?

GILES. Not of enough matter to be worth naming.
Brother Giles, they call me.

BEGGAR. Giles is an ill name.   I knew a man
named Giles, was hanged for it.

GILES. Because he was named Giles ?

BEGGAR. Aye.   There was another named Giles
had done that which he was hanged for.   So his
name hanged him.

GILES. Who were *you* hanging just now ?

BEGGAR. I ?   I was hanging nobody.

GILES. Oh, yes, you were, Brother ;   and with a
will—had there been rope enough.   [*He holds out
his hand for the cloth.*]   Come ;   was it that he made
this too short, that you cursed him ?

BEGGAR. Oh ?   *That* fool ?

GILES. Show it me.

BEGGAR. That won't cover my legs.   And 'twas
my legs that wanted covering.

GILES. It will, if you kneel down, Brother.

BEGGAR. I ?   Kneel ?   If I did, I 'd never get
up again !

GILES. There is the making of a good end, Brother.

BEGGAR. Stop your ' brothering ' ! I 'm not your brother. I should think you 'd a flea for your father, from the look of you !

GILES. Very likely, Brother—little Father, I mean. . . . Who gave you this cloak ?

BEGGAR. 'Tis not a cloak ; 'tis but the half of one.

GILES. Yet it is a cloak in the making, if I give you the rest of it.

[*He goes back to his bench and picks up the cloak which lies there.*

BEGGAR [*contemptuous of his benefactors*]. Oh ! Here 's another of 'em.

GILES [*measuring piece against piece*]. Let me see : where should it begin ?

BEGGAR [*quick to the situation*]. The top half, with the hood to it, mind ! What he gave me was but the bottom half.

GILES [*nodding and smiling*]. The top half as you say, Brother. [*And he continues his measuring.*] Brother Rufus, have you a knife or scissors about you ?

RUFUS. I have only my teeth, Brother ; and yours are better. If you bite through the hem, you can tear the rest easily.

BEGGAR [*impatiently*]. Here, fools ! What 'll you be tearing up two for, to make one ? You 've only to give me the top half, and swap me the bottom half : then I get a cloak, and the thing 's done.

GILES. Very true. What a brain you have, Brother ! [*Keeping the half cloak, he gives him his own.*] This saves making, or mending. As you say, the thing is done. . . . Who gave you this, did you say ?

BEGGAR [*as he arrays himself*]. Do you know a greater fool in the world than yourself ?

GILES. No.

BEGGAR. Well, it was him, then.

RUFUS. That 'll be Brother Juniper, I 'm thinking.

GILES. No : Juniper would have been wiser. He would have given all, not half.

BEGGAR. Aye : so he would, if he had not given the other half to a leper. . . . I could kill that leper !

GILES. No need now, Brother.

RUFUS. So 'twas Brother Juniper, was it ? That 's the third gone this month.

GILES [*kissing it*]. O cloak of Brother Juniper ! Were a king to come now and offer me his robe in exchange, I would not take it. Little Father, I thank you for your good bounty. This is better for me.

BEGGAR. Say no more, then ! If both be suited, there is less to complain of. Now I must haste, for I have business.

GILES. God prosper it, Brother. If you have further need, come and tell me.

[*He returns to his work-bench.*

BEGGAR. Oh, do not fear ! To-night I shall be rich.

RUFUS. Rich ? How, Brother ?

BEGGAR. Have ye not heard, the King of France comes here to-day ?

RUFUS. The King of France ? Why, what brings him ?

183

BEGGAR. His horse, I suppose. That, and the Pope's orders. He goes to the Holy Land to fight for our Lord's deliverance from King Herod, and from Pontiff Pilate. . . . I thought King Herod was dead.

RUFUS. He won't stay here.

BEGGAR. He will pass through. And they say that, every city he enters, he gives such alms, beggars are made rich by it. But I don't wait here for him : I shall out to meet him. When he comes I shall strip myself naked—as a sign of humility. Then, if he make me not rich, God make him a leper ! . . . Farewell, fool-brother !

GILES. Farewell ! God bless you in your riches, Brother.

[*The* BEGGAR *goes, and* GILES *continues his hammering.* RUFUS *takes up the half cloak, and begins handling it.*

RUFUS. 'Tis said he is a wondrously good man—that some day he is like to become a saint.

GILES. Yonder poor old beggar, do you say ? I should not wonder.

RUFUS. No, no, Brother. The King of France, I meant : ' good King Louis,' as they call him.

GILES. 'Tis a name of sweet savour. One of our Brothers, lately out of France, brought us a gentle message from him—because we are followers ; and all that he then told of him was good. [*Then, as* RUFUS *throws down the cloak beside him.*] Hey, Brother ! when Juniper returns, he will be needing a new cloak. Canst thou find him one ?

RUFUS. I can make one for him : or one for thee.

GILES. Not for me, Brother ; but for him as

184

quickly as thou canst, else for pity I shall be tempted to give this back to him. Now must I make it so that I can wear it.

[*He takes up the cloak, and is about to go.*

RUFUS. Sew thyself into it, Brother ; else thou wilt lose it—as did Juniper.

[*The going of* BROTHER GILES *is arrested by the entrance of* BROTHER HUMBLE, *who comes running, very eager and out of breath.*

HUMBLE. Have you heard ? O Brothers, have you heard ? The great King of France is here, in this city ; and men be all about, seeking him !

RUFUS. Oh ? So the old beggar was right, was he ?

HUMBLE. Did you know, Brothers ?

RUFUS. Only what was told us—that they were expecting him.

HUMBLE. He was here before any knew of it. Shall we not go, Brothers, and see him ?

RUFUS [*discouragingly*]. There will be enough to see him without us, Brother.

[HUMBLE *stands disappointed and abashed.*

GILES [*kindly*]. Run, Brother, run : and when you have seen him—you will have seen him.

[*For a moment* HUMBLE *stands hesitating ; but now others are running down the street with cries of excitement, and catching the infection he runs too.*

RUFUS [*with a grunt*]. If he be not back for his bell-ringing, there 'll be trouble.

GILES [*now on his way out*]. We can do it for him, Brother.

RUFUS. What does he want to see a king for ?

[*There is no answer* : GILES *has gone.* RUFUS
*takes up two pitchers of water and prepares
to follow him. Then up from the street, in
the hood and cloak of a pilgrim, comes* KING
LOUIS, *followed by an* Attendant Squire. *At
a signal from* LOUIS, *his companion goes
across and touches* RUFUS *on the shoulder.*
RUFUS *turns.*

LOUIS. Are you the Brother that I spoke with ?

RUFUS. At the gate, Signor ? A covered knight
spoke to me, but his face I could not see.

LOUIS. It was I. Was it here you said that I
should find Brother Giles ? Is this his house ?

RUFUS. He has no house, Signor ; but he lives
here.

LOUIS. Bring me to him, quickly ; or him to me.

RUFUS. Who shall I say, Signor ?

LOUIS. My name does not matter. ' A friend,'
tell him ; one that has long desired to see him.

RUFUS. Ah ? So you know him, Signor ?

LOUIS. I shall know him—when I see him.

RUFUS. I will go, Signor.

[*He goes.*

SQUIRE. He does not know you, my lord.

LOUIS. How should he, friend ? Here, all alike,
we are strangers.

SQUIRE. Not so much all alike, my lord, as you
did wish. The Podesta had caught the news, and
was there waiting.

LOUIS. Nevertheless we escaped him.

SQUIRE. I think only for a time, my lord.

LOUIS. 'Twill be time enough, friend. For to see
this little Brother is all I come for.

SQUIRE. I had never heard of him, my lord.

LOUIS. And I—have never seen him. . . . Oh, there ! See ! There he is !

[*The cry is uttered before* GILES *has actually appeared. Now he comes, followed by* RUFUS.

SQUIRE. Are you so sure of him, my lord ?

[*But between* LOUIS *and* BROTHER GILES *there is no room for doubt. Almost simultaneously, as for the first time their eyes meet, there breaks from each a cry of profound joy and satisfaction. One moment they stand at gaze ; the next, with welcoming gesture, run together and embrace. Three times they embrace ; then, with linked and extended arms, remain looking at each other, in a deep communion of love. For a while* RUFUS *stands watching them with grave and considerate regard ; then gently approaching the* King's *Companion, who waits at the threshold, he speaks.*

RUFUS. Your friend, Signor, has found a welcome. Will not you also come in and rest ?

SQUIRE. I am content to stay here, Brother. And *your* friend—who is he ?

RUFUS. That is Brother Giles. It must have been long since they met.

SQUIRE. Never before, Brother.

RUFUS [*astonished*]. Who, then, or what is he ?

SQUIRE [*after a pause*]. My master.

RUFUS. One, surely with a good heart, and of great understanding ?

SQUIRE. He has both, Brother. . . . But here is something we understand not.

RUFUS. Look how they join—like brothers !

SQUIRE. Of one race. Say, was this Brother of yours not born—a prince ?

RUFUS. No, Signor : only a poor man, like all the rest of us.

[*A bell has struck the hour. In the distance a trumpet sounds.*

SQUIRE. Strange : oh, most strange ! . . . What can it mean ?

RUFUS. I think, Signor, they are lovers.

SQUIRE. Strangers, that know each other !

RUFUS. Indeed, it would seem so.

[*Cell doors open. The* FATHER MINISTER *enters. Others of the* Brethren *follow.*

FATHER MINISTER [*to the first who enters*]. How is this, Brother ? The hour has gone, but there is no bell for us.

RUFUS. Brother Humble has gone out, Father Minister. I will ring it for him.

Enter BROTHER HUMBLE, *running.*

HUMBLE. There ! there ! I 'm late ; and now he 'll be gone, and I shan't see him ! Oh, dear, dear, dear !

[*He takes the bell-rope, and begins ringing. Brothers begin to come in, halting at sight of the lovers who still stand in silent embrace. Down below in the city, a trumpet sounds three times.* LOUIS *and* BROTHER GILES *draw apart, each making upon the other the sign of the Cross.*

SQUIRE. See, now they are parting !

RUFUS [*also crossing himself*]. Pacem aeternam dona eis, Domine ! Et lux perpetua luceat eis.

[LOUIS *and* BROTHER GILES *have embraced for
the last time. As they part*, GILES *turns and
goes quickly up to his cell*, LOUIS *back to his*
Companion.

LOUIS. Take my hand quick, and lead me, for I
am blind ! The trumpet signals for us ; and we
must go. Ah ! Friend ! Where art thou ?

SQUIRE. My lord, I was too full for speaking.
Have hold of me, and come !

[*As, with joined hands, they go out*, BROTHER
JUNIPER *enters. He turns and looks at them.*

JUNIPER. Oh ? So he 's been here, has he : the
wise man ! The Lord bless it to him !

RUFUS. He ? Who ?

[*Again a trumpet is thrice blown.*

JUNIPER. Yonder man—just gone out.

FATHER MINISTER. Do you know him, Brother ?

JUNIPER. Know him ? Didn't ye hear the
trumpets ? Don't ye hear 'em now ? Who is it
has trumpets blown for him ?

FATHER MINISTER. Well, who, then ?

JUNIPER. Sure : the King of France ; who else ?

ALL. The King of France !

JUNIPER [*pointing*]. That quiet-going man yonder,
under the grey cloak, is him.

[*They all crowd to look* ; BROTHER HUMBLE,
turning, sees BROTHER GILES, *back from his
cell, with his shoe-mendings in his hand.*

HUMBLE. Brother Giles, dost thou hear ? Didst
thou know ?

SEVERAL. Tell us, Brother Giles : tell us !

[*They all gather round him.*

GILES. What is it, Brothers ?

FATHER MINISTER. That was the King of France, Brother!

GILES. Happy France!

FATHER MINISTER. Didst thou *know*?

GILES. Yes, Father; when I saw him, I knew—though how, I know not; for I looked not to his head, but only to his heart.

> [*Vexed, and bewildered, the* Brothers *all begin talking together, none waiting till another has finished.*

THE BROTHERS [*together and disjointedly*]. But why came he? What said he? Did you not speak to him; nor he to you? And knowing all the time, you let him go, without telling us? And he a great king, doing us so great an honour! And you treating him like a brother and an equal! Why, Brother Giles, how wast thou not afraid?

GILES. Why should I fear one that I love?

RUFUS. But why, then, didst thou not speak to him?

GILES [*giving the shoes*]. Here are my mendings, Juniper. . . . Why should I speak, Brother? Words are no use, save to show what is in men's minds. But when he and I had looked on each other, we needed no words to tell us anything. That I loved him, that he loved me, was plain: that we had in our hearts no separate desire was plain also. We had but to look at each other . . . it was enough.

JUNIPER. The little Brother is right, Brothers! And had he made this as right, I wouldn't be talking, either. But there, look! Call you that a mending?

> [*He pulls off the patch as he speaks.*

GILES. I'm sorry, Brother; I'm sorry!

JUNIPER. Oh, you 've a great heart, but you are a bad shoemaker ! . . . Come ! I 'll show you.

[*So saying,* JUNIPER *leads the way back to the work-bench, and sits down on it.*

FATHER MINISTER. Leave them together, Brothers. They are a pair, and we cannot mend them.

[*And as it is for a meal that the bell has summoned them, the* Brethren *all pass out to the adjoining refectory.* JUNIPER *sorts out his tools, and begins cutting and hammering.* GILES, *standing behind, leans over with affectionate embrace, and watches him.* JUNIPER *looks up to explain.*

JUNIPER. I 'm thinking of the poor fellow that 's got to wear them.

GILES. They are mine, Brother.

JUNIPER. Sure ! I know that. . . . Now, look, and learn something ! Else, if there 's shoemaking in Heaven, they won't put *you* to it ! . . . That 's sure.

[*He returns to business, and* BROTHER GILES *resumes his interrupted song.*

GILES.

A light the manger lit ;
    There lay the Mother meek.
Said they, ' This place is fit :
    Here is the rest we seek.'

They loosed their latchet strings ;
    So stood they all unshod.
Come in, ye kings, ye kings,
    And kiss the Feet of God !

[*Far away in the distance a trumpet is blown*

thrice. BROTHER GILES *stands upright to listen.* BROTHER JUNIPER *stops, turns, looks up at him, and sees his face tender and full of radiance. Laying down his tool, he takes hold of* BROTHER GILES' *sleeve and kisses it; then resumes his hammering.*

[*Again, more distantly, the trumpet is blown.*

CURTAIN

NOTE

'ST. LOUIS, King of France, hearing the exceeding great fame of Brother Giles, determined at all costs to visit him personally; for which reason he came to Perugia, where the said Brother Giles lived at that time. And coming to the door of the community-house, as an unknown pilgrim, he asked for Brother Giles, not telling the porter who he was that asked. The porter therefore went to Brother Giles, and told him there was a pilgrim at the door asking for him; wherefor immediately, with great fervour of spirit, he came out of his cell and ran to the door; and without further questioning and without even having seen each other before, with the greatest devotion inclining themselves, they embraced and kissed one another with such familiarity as though for a long while they had been together in intimate friendship. But with all this neither one nor the other spoke; but they stood thus embracing each other, with this sign of the love of charity between them, in silence. And after they had stood thus a great space without either speaking a word to the other, they departed from each other, and St. Louis went on his journey and Brother Giles returned to his cell.'

Little Flowers of St. Francis.

THE FOOL'S ERRAND

(1243)

At his bench in the Community-house at Perugia, BROTHER JUNIPER *sits cobbling a pair of shoes. He is now an old man; but in spite of its ugliness his face is still rather like a child's, with its look of foolish innocence which nothing can change. To-day there is an added expression of dazed wonder, as of one who has seen vision or ghost, and is not quite sure which; and while he hammers the leather upon his block, timing word to blow, he talks to himself.*

JUNIPER. I am ! . . . I am ! . . . I am ! . . .

    [BROTHER GILES, *descending the stairs, hears him, halts in the doorway for a moment, peeps curiously, then advances.*

GILES. What are you saying ' I am ' for, Brother ?

JUNIPER. Sure, to remind myself.

GILES. What of ?

JUNIPER. That I 'm Brother Juniper—the fool.

GILES. What should make you forget it, Brother ?

JUNIPER. Huh ! I 've had enough happen to me to-day to make me forget anything. [*He resumes his hammering.*] I am ! . . . I am ! . . . I am ! . . .

    [GILES *watches him patiently awhile, then speaks.*

GILES. Are you going to tell me, Brother ?

JUNIPER. If I start talking, I'll never stop myself; and here's a shoe to be mended that can't wait.

GILES. You talk, Brother, while I mend it.

JUNIPER [*with affectionate contempt*]. You ? . . . I'll have to watch you. . . . D'you know a welt when you see it ?

GILES. I've mended my own shoes, Brother— you having taught me. There ! Look at them !

[*Seating himself beside* JUNIPER, *he lifts his feet for inspection, then gently but firmly begins to oust* JUNIPER *from his place.*

JUNIPER [*after inspecting the shoes*]. Well, it isn't in mortal sin you did that. I'll forgive you. . . . But I'm going to keep my eye on you ; mind that !

GILES [*taking up the shoes*]. Yes, Brother. Now begin !

[*Suddenly* JUNIPER *delivers himself explosively.*

JUNIPER. Laugh !

[BROTHER GILES *yields himself heartily to the provocation. Sight of* JUNIPER'S *grim earnestness keeps him going. Then, sobering to business, he takes up his task ; but* JUNIPER *has not yet done with him.*

JUNIPER. Now cry !

[*At this* GILES *laughs the more.* JUNIPER, *with a lenient kick, while reiterating his command, calls him to order.*

JUNIPER. On holy obedience I tell you to cry.

[GILES *does his best, but makes a poor show of it.*

JUNIPER. You laugh better than you cry ; but you mean well. Now for it !

[*He pauses, ruminates, takes a breath, and begins.*

194

JUNIPER. I was sitting here. . . . You 'll cry in good earnest, before I 've done telling you ! . . .

> [GILES *is wise, and makes no answer to the challenge. But* JUNIPER *still has a difficulty in getting started, and dropping the tone of narrative, turns to question.*

JUNIPER. Have you ever been tempted of the Devil, Brother ?

GILES. Very often.

JUNIPER. What d'you do for it ?

GILES. I do as our Lord did : I tell him to get behind me.

JUNIPER. Does he ?

GILES. Sometimes yes : sometimes no.

JUNIPER. Ah ! Our Lord can do it ; but I can't trust myself when I 've got the Devil behind me. . . . Why ? Because I 'm weak in the back. . . . No ; what I do is make him go in front of me. I put him in blinkers ; I give him a heavy load ; I tell him I 'll be kind to him ; I tell him if he 'll go where I want him I 'll do him a service ; then, when I 've got him well on the trot, I just leave him. And with him not looking behind, and me not looking in front, before he 's got there we 've parted company—for that time, at any rate. . . . That 's my way, Brother.

GILES. Where do you tell him to go, Juniper ?

JUNIPER. Tell him to go to Hell, of course.

GILES. How do you load him ?

JUNIPER. With kindness and compassion. He doesn't like it.

GILES. And what service do you do him ?

JUNIPER. Getting him back to Hell where he 's

come from, and where he wants to be. He gets a rest there—from tempting people : the only place where he does. . . . Has it ever struck you, Brother Giles, that if the Devil stayed in Hell he 'd be sinless ?

GILES. Sinless, Brother ?

JUNIPER. Harming nobody.

GILES. But in Hell, Brother, pride, and wrath, and envy do still devour him ; he hates God, loves darkness, seeks power to do evil.

JUNIPER. Ah ; you 've answered me ! Give me back my mendings : I 'm no good at talking.

GILES. No, no, Brother ; for 'twas not that you meant to tell me—was it ?

JUNIPER. I meant to tell you how the Devil came tempting me, just ; and how it all turned to blessing. Ah ! the Lord 'll crack him out of his misery, someday, we 'll pray !—like you do for a flea— for he does good sometimes without knowing it.

GILES. Yes ; but go on, Brother.

[*Thus pulled up,* JUNIPER *sits, thinks, and begins again.*

JUNIPER. Do you remember, Brother Giles, how, when Father Francis was alive, I would always be doing things that seemed wrong, and that he said was right ; but that others said wasn't right ?

[GILES *nods, smiling at certain recollections as he does so.*

JUNIPER. Now when 'twas always like that, how was one to know ? What was one to do ?

GILES. Trust Father Francis.

JUNIPER. I did that. But he, twenty years dead and gone to glory, whom am I to trust now ?

GILES. Yourself, Brother.

JUNIPER. The Lord forgive me !—that's what I'm going to do. Now I'll tell you. . . .

[*He comes again to a full stop, and starts fresh.*

JUNIPER. When you go to see our Holy Father the Pope, sitting on his throne, d'you lie on your flat, and kiss his toe ; or d'you only—— ?

GILES. I have never seen the Holy Father on his throne, Brother.

JUNIPER. But if you did, should you take off your shoes and go barefoot ? Should you spit on yourself first, and say ' What a worm am I ! ' or should you leave him to do it ?

GILES [*doing his best to keep grave*]. I should leave him to do it, Brother.

JUNIPER. Sure, that 'd be a great honour !

GILES. Yes, Brother. But has what you were to tell me anything to do with the Pope ?

JUNIPER. Yes ; it 's got everything to do with him.

GILES. Then go on.

JUNIPER. Where was I ?

GILES. Not at the beginning yet, so far as I can see.

JUNIPER. Indeed, then, I am ! Didn't I tell you the Devil tempted me ?

GILES. You did, Brother. How did he tempt you ?

[JUNIPER *becomes solemn ; his voice sinks to awe.*

JUNIPER. By fear ! . . . Fear !

GILES [*properly impressed*]. Fear ?

[JUNIPER *gives an endorsing grunt ; then, after a further pause, gathers resolution and begins.*

JUNIPER. I was sitting here, Brother : just where

I am now; when I saw some one coming. He was too far off for me to tell what kind or like he was—except that he wasn't a woman. But the way he walked reminded me just of the only man I used to fear. . . .

GILES [*after waiting*]. Who was that, Brother ?

JUNIPER [*after more waiting*]. Father Elias.

[*At that name the compassionate heart of* BROTHER GILES *heaves a sigh.*

GILES. You did well to fear him, Brother; for he has sinned grievously against the Faith; he is out of the Order; Rome has excommunicated him.

JUNIPER. I know it, Brother.

GILES. As our Father Francis—taught by vision —foretold.

JUNIPER. Yes, Brother.

GILES. So now, when he dies, he will be damned.

JUNIPER. No, Brother.

GILES. No ? But what can save him, Brother ?

JUNIPER. Do you not remember how the little Father prayed, and got fresh mercy for him; and told him that, though he must die out of the Order, he need not, for all that, be damned ?

GILES. If he repented.

JUNIPER. He has repented.

GILES. How do you know ? . . . How can you be sure ?

JUNIPER. Because—that was him, Brother.

GILES. Who ?

JUNIPER. The man whose walk reminded me. . . . The man that—as I saw coming—I felt afraid.

GILES. He : Father Elias—came here !

JUNIPER. Here, where I am now.

GILES. Why did he come?

JUNIPER [*the wonder of it not yet gone for him*]. To see me, Brother. . . . I am! . . . I am! . . . I am! . . . 'Twas then the Devil tempted me: for when I saw him coming, and *knew*, I was afraid, and tried to run and hide myself. . . . I did that. And he just came to the door, and waited—waited: didn't knock, didn't come in. There was he; and there was I. [*He indicates the corner beyond the window.*] Oh, what wickedness possessed me to be afraid of him—now!

GILES. Why did he come to see you, Brother?

JUNIPER. To ask me to pray for him. . . . Now! [*in challenging tone*] are you going to laugh, or are you going to cry? [*Suddenly his voice grows tender.*] Look, Brother; Father Elias has had his head there on my knee!—Father Elias! . . . [*His voice rises with passion.*] And I tell God that if Father Elias could put his head on Brother Juniper's knee, he's a different man—to the man he was! And I'm going to tell Father Pope the same. . . . I am! . . . I am! . . . I am! . . .

[BROTHER GILES *lays down his work, and reaches out a hand to* BROTHER JUNIPER.

GILES. Brother Juniper. . . .

[*Tears rush to his eyes; he can say no more.*

JUNIPER. Ah! I thought you wouldn't laugh when I told you; and I don't blame you. What I want to know is: if he's such a different man—what am I?

GILES [*tenderly*]. You are the same, Brother—as always.

JUNIPER. The fool?

GILES. The fool. . . . That is why he came, Brother. . . . Do you remember, Juniper, how once the little Father bade you to stay : because, he said, Father Elias needed you ?

JUNIPER. I do, Brother !

[*He sits rapt in wonder.*

GILES. Because ' where wisdom and prudence are the rule,' he said, ' fools are precious.'

JUNIPER. Sure ; yes, I remember !

GILES. So now it has come true. The little Father was wise, Juniper.

JUNIPER. The Lord help me to be good for him ! . . I 'm going to try.

GILES [*with diffidence*]. Tell me, Brother, what he said to you ; if you may tell me.

JUNIPER. He said nothing, Brother, but just to tell me what he was : lonely, and weary ; and without a hope ; full of hate of what he had done ; full of sorrow for his sins ; all his pride gone. . . . He was humble, Brother. Almost it made me afraid of him again, to see him so humble—afraid if I touched I 'd hurt. ' Brother Juniper, pray for me ! ' was all he said. But how he said it ; oh, how he said it !

GILES. And you ?

JUNIPER. Little enough could I do—being but a fool. Sure, I kissed him, Brother : he let me ! But he didn't kiss—*me*. [*Again the wonder takes him ; he pauses, and then goes on.*] Then he got up—and went.

GILES. Where to, Brother ?

JUNIPER. To the Leper-house.

GILES [*shuddering*]. Alas ! has he also become a leper?

JUNIPER. No. He 's gone there, because there, he

said, they 'll let an outcast do service. I offered he
should come here; but he wouldn't!—because he 's
under excommunication. . . . 'Brother Juniper,
pray for me!' he says. . . . I 've been doing it
ever since. And now I 've something else to do.
That 's why I was mending those shoes.

GILES. His, Brother?

JUNIPER. No; mine. I 've a long journey before me.

GILES. Where are you going?

JUNIPER. To Rome, Brother. . . . Is it laugh
now, or cry? . . . I 'm going to see the Holy
Father. . . . I 'm going to tell him what I know.
. . . I 'm going to ask him—for what Father
Francis promised, to come true. . . . And I 'm
not afraid of the Pope, now, Brother. . . . I 'm
afraid of nobody. . . . Why? Because I 've had
Brother Elias come to me—here, to *me*; and say—
but I can't say it as he said it : 'Brother Juniper,
pray for me!' And 'Brother Juniper,' he says,
'ask our blessed Father Francis to pray for me.'
. . . I ! . . . I ! . . . Can you believe?

GILES. I can well, Brother.

JUNIPER. Aye; you 've the brain for it. I
haven't. . . . But I 'm praying hard; for I 'd like
Father Francis to know.

GILES. Doubtless he does know, Brother.

JUNIPER. And I 'd like—Sister Clare to know.

GILES. She shall know, Brother.

JUNIPER. And there 's one other. [*There is a
long pause.* GILES *waits patiently.*] I 'd like—
Brother Leo to know.

GILES. Alas! where he is we know not.

JUNIPER. But God knows. . . . When Father Elias turned him out of the Order—it wasn't right, Brother—was it ?

GILES. No.

JUNIPER. . . . So there's Brother Elias ; and there's Brother Leo ; and here am I. . . . And I going to tell the Pope—for both of 'em !

GILES. May I come with you, Brother ?

JUNIPER. No, Brother. I'm going to do this alone. I'm not afraid. . . . [*He rises.*] There ! Talking's over. Give back : I must get on with those shoes. I've got to wear 'em.

[GILES *rises, kisses the shoes as he returns them, and goes to draw water.*

JUNIPER. Oh ! there's another at it again ! All fools every one of us ! . . . I am ! . . . I am ! . . . I am !

GILES [*singing as he draws the water*].

Praised be my Lord for all fools,
    And namely praise for our Brother Ass :
The ways of the wise He overrules ;
    And mighty things He bringeth to pass.

JUNIPER [*busy at his mendings again*]. I am !

[*His pitcher filled,* GILES *turns to look at* JUNIPER, *then goes slowly up the stairs.*

GILES. Praised be my Lord for all who give
    Pardon to others for His love's sake ;
And meekly endure in pains to live :
    In Him they rest, and in Him shall wake.

[*His voice dies away as he turns the stair.* JUNIPER *continues his mendings.*

CURTAIN

THE LAST COMMENT

 BROTHER JUNIPER's *bed has been made for him in a room adjoining the chapel of the Friary, so that from there he may hear the Holy Office each day. A closed-up arch-way in the wall indicates that what is now two was once one. Old and worn, he lies with eyes shut ; but opens them and turns his head when —the watching Brother having made way for her—*SISTER GIACOMINA *comes and sits down by the bed. Slowly, and with surprise at the admission of a woman to the Friary, he recognises her comfortable presence. They touch hands.*

JUNIPER. Have they let you in, Sister ?

GIACOMINA [*with humorous significance in her tone*]. I have come in, Brother.

JUNIPER. Isn't that against the rules, Sister dear ?

GIACOMINA. An exception to the rule, Brother. But the rule was made *for* us, not against us. Were it not so, 'twould have no meaning.

JUNIPER [*sadly*]. Since the rule 's been altered from what the little Father made it, it 's had a hard meaning for me.

GIACOMINA. Rules often are hard, Brother : 'tis their nature.

JUNIPER. And now—I 'm done with it.

GIACOMINA. Having done well with it.

JUNIPER. And I 'm wondering—if there 's as many rules in Heaven as there is for getting there —whether I 'll ever get so as to understand 'em. . . . And if I don't, Sister . . . ?

GIACOMINA. The little Father is there, Brother, to explain them.

JUNIPER [*with a deep breath of restful wonder*]. The little Father ! . . . Seeing him again, in his glory, shall I know him ?

GIACOMINA. Surely ; why, surely !

JUNIPER. Eh ! What 's a sinner like me got to be sure about ?

GIACOMINA. Love, Brother.

JUNIPER. Ah, you 've answered me ! We be sure of that, anyhow, through knowing *him*. . . . A wonderful love his was : made you so sure that where that came from—there must be more of it. And yet there 's millions of us, all through the world, that have eyes—looking, and seeing nothing ! . . . What are you thinking there, all by yourself, Sister ? . . . What are you smiling for ?

GIACOMINA. Because life is beautiful. Could we but see *how* beautiful, we also should see what lies beyond—as he did.

JUNIPER. What 'll it be, d' ye think ? Eh, Sister ?

GIACOMINA. More life, Brother ; and then more ! and then—still more.

JUNIPER. Eh, but different.

GIACOMINA. Without death : yes. But for all that, very much the same.

JUNIPER. As what we 're seeing now ?

GIACOMINA. As what we are *not* seeing ; but is here with us all the time.

JUNIPER. The little Father : we saw *him*—quite plain—didn't we ?

GIACOMINA. Some more plainly than others : you better than most.

JUNIPER. Ah, the sight he was to me ! And wasn't it a mercy and a God's wonder that I should see him, for all I was made so foolish ?

GIACOMINA. Every good has mercy and wonder in it, Brother.

JUNIPER. Eh ! but it had to dig deep to find *me*.

GIACOMINA. No ; you were there, ready, waiting for it. The first time you saw him, did you not love him ?

JUNIPER. Sure ! and you there, too, Sister ! D' ye not remember ?

GIACOMINA. Yes, Brother.

JUNIPER. And what like, first time, was he to you, Sister ?

GIACOMINA. I was at his father's house, buying cloth. He was serving me. A beggar came asking alms in God's name. The little Father told him to go away.

JUNIPER [*amazed*]. He did that ?

GIACOMINA. He was but a boy, then. He went on serving me. All at once he threw up his hands : he was in tears. Leaving me, he ran after the beggar, gave him for his need, knelt, kissed his hand. . . . That is how I first saw him, Brother— first knew him ; thereafter remembered him.

Four years later—you with us—we met again.
Seeing him once, who could ever forget him ?

JUNIPER. Not you or I, Sister. But there's
others. . . . Lying here, thinking — I've been
troubled—troubled.

GIACOMINA. Why, Brother ?

JUNIPER. Because *they'll* forget. They won't
all remember him like we do.

GIACOMINA. No, Brother ; but for all that, the
little Father will still be remembered. Even the
world, though it goes not his way, will not forget
him.

JUNIPER. But there's things he did, that you
and I know—I more of 'em than you, maybe, for
being oftener with him—that, when we're gone,
'll get forgotten—such beautiful things, Sister
they oughtn't just die with us when we die !

GIACOMINA. They won't, Brother.

JUNIPER. How not ?

GIACOMINA. In ways we can't see. Coming into
the lives of others, there they sow seed ; and the
seed lives and quickens, though whence sprung it
knows not.

JUNIPER. But it all ought to be known. And
if men were but wiser, and had more love in 'em,
wouldn't they have cared so to get it said and
written that never could it get lost like it's going
to be ? Here am I—such a fool as never was nor
will be in the world again—and yet I'm full of
precious things that nobody knows of ! And when
I'm gone, they're gone : aye, to seed, maybe ;
but the shape of it, and the touch of it, and the
sound of it won't be the same ever again.

THE LAST COMMENT

GIACOMINA. Life never stays the same, Brother ; growth changes it.

JUNIPER. Aye, but you keep telling of it. And when you can—and it's worth it—you get some one to write it all down for you. But for that, we'd never have had the Gospels telling us of our Lord.

GIACOMINA. No ; that's true, Brother. You are right.

JUNIPER. So here am I, knowing so much, and remembering it all ; but such a fool that when I begin trying to tell of it—it doesn't come right, Sister. But it's all *here* ; and here's he, that I've so got hold of him he can't let me go. I haven't the right mind, nor the right words for it : but it's him—the very life of him—here in this poor body, going back to the dust ! . . . That's the only reason I've got, Sister, for not wishing to die.

GIACOMINA. But all that—you will take with you, Brother.

JUNIPER. Where it's not wanted like as it is here. . . . I've done so little for everybody—the poor world the little Father loved so : I wish, now it's come to the last, I could just empty myself out of all I know of him. But I can't !

GIACOMINA. You have, more than you guess, Brother.

JUNIPER. It must have been the same—what I'm so wishing now—with our Lord's own disciples ; simple men some of 'em, that couldn't write anything. Twelve : and for all that they've told us so much, think of all the lot more that'll never be told—things that God Himself did on earth! If only we could know what He did then, when they stop telling us—the next little thing, no matter how little it might be : only a kind word, maybe, to a poor, down-laden beast, or a child that had broke something and was crying over it ; or what He said to His Mother times when He went home again : what He said first thing in the morning when she came to wake Him ; how He comforted her when dear Saint Father Joseph was dead. And all His learning of things when He was a child : everyday things like that, done by God Himself, that men have forgotten ! It doesn't seem right, Sister.

GIACOMINA. But it is right, Brother ; and never has God willed it to be otherwise. It is so that we all live our lives ; we ourselves do not know, cannot remember all that has gone to make us what we are. We are brought to birth, grow, enter the common heritage, die hence, and are forgotten. For all lives that has been the way since life began. But—these helping—man is still in the making ; and God in His good time will make us all to be one.

JUNIPER. Yes . . . I suppose. But it wants faith to be sure of it.

GIACOMINA. You will not have to wait long to be sure now, Brother. Trust God—only for one more day. [*She pauses ; there is no answer.*] Is that—difficult ?

[*Again there is a pause ; then with sorrowful self-accusation* JUNIPER *speaks.*

JUNIPER. Dark !

GIACOMINA. Are you afraid of the dark, Brother ?

JUNIPER. I am, where I find it, Sister—in myself. That 's where I 'm dark. ' Get rid of self,' he said : but I haven't done it.

GIACOMINA. Not quite ; almost.

[*The watching* Brother *has returned, and standing in the door makes a sign.* GIACOMINA *rises.*

Yes, Brother ; must I go ?

BROTHER. It 's the Angelus, Sister.

GIACOMINA [*to* JUNIPER]. Take up your weariness, and rest, Brother. Have no fear. Sleep ! God give you peace.

JUNIPER. Are you going ? Are you leaving me, Sister dear ?

GIACOMINA. Not very far ; not very long, Brother. We shall meet again.

JUNIPER [*reaching out to hold her*]. Soon, eh ?

GIACOMINA. In God's time. The order which we must obey has come for both of us. Go to sleep, Brother.

[*Meanwhile the* BROTHER SACRISTAN *has entered, and crossing quickly to the further door, is there seen ringing the Angelus.* GIACOMINA *and the two* Brothers *recite the ' Ave Maria ' together.* JUNIPER, *already drowsing, does not join in, but as the last stroke of the bell dies away, he speaks.*

JUNIPER. Sister Bell has a sweet sound . . . little Father. [*He goes to sleep.*]

[*Having rung the Angelus, the* Sacristan *returns to the door and stands waiting.*

GIACOMINA. Yes, Brother : in one moment.

WATCHER. He is asleep, Sister.

GIACOMINA. What ? Obedient, so soon ? [*She kneels at the foot of the bed.*] O little Brother, simple and foolish, but wise : when thou comest of thy simplicity to the bright light of God, pray for me and for all sinners, that we also may become wise through Love !

> [*She rises and goes silently out. The* Watcher *sits down by the bed; his eyes are heavy with sleep, his head droops. Meantime, in the adjoining chapel the singing of the Office has begun. It gets dark; a* Brother *enters carrying two tapers; he pauses and gazes down on the sleeping* JUNIPER, *looks across at the other* Brother, *now asleep also, and passes through. Presently the singing of the Office becomes blended with a low vibration of sound, which merges gradually into the quick but muffled tolling of a bell, the urgency of its summons subdued by distance and the thickness of walls. Slowly the darkened chamber where* JUNIPER *lies asleep becomes filled with the figment of his dream. Amid the seated ranks of this shadowy tribunal, one form higher than the rest sits darkly enthroned. What light there is comes from behind, so that no face is seen. Presently from the seat of judgment comes the* Voice *of the presiding authority.*

VOICE. Brother Juniper.

> [JUNIPER *does not move, but his eyes open, and he answers in a voice faint with awe.*

JUNIPER. Yes, Father.

VOICE. Stand out where all may look on thee !

JUNIPER. Yes, Father. . . . But I can't, Father.

VOICE. Wherefor ?

JUNIPER. I 'm here, tied by the leg, Father. And on holy obedience I 'm not to sit up till they tell me.

VOICE. Hear, then, and answer ! What hast thou done with thy life, Brother ?

JUNIPER. I don't know, Father. . . . Nothing, Father.

VOICE. Nothing ?

JUNIPER. Nothing well enough that I ought to have done, Father. Many things well enough that I shouldn't have done.

VOICE. How ' well '—things that you should not ?

JUNIPER. Well enough to please the Devil, Father.

VOICE. Many have complained of thee.

JUNIPER. The Lord help, heal, and keep them all from the hurt I 've done to them !

VOICE. Doubt not He will, Brother ; the better if thou art now penitent.

JUNIPER. Sure, I 'm penitent for everything. I 'd be penitent of being born ; but God won't let me. It would be wrong, wouldn't it, Father ? . . . And besides . . .

VOICE. Yea, speak !

JUNIPER. If I hadn't been born, I shouldn't have known the little Father.

VOICE. The little Father was not God, Brother. Thou wast born to know and worship God—not man, His creature.

JUNIPER. I should never have come to know Him, but for the little Father.

VOICE. Why ?   Wast thou blind ?

JUNIPER. No ;   only a fool, Father.   But *he* loved, he knew, he made me understand.

VOICE. Is he here with thee—now ?

JUNIPER. Aye. . . . But it 's dark . . . and down here is temptation.

VOICE. Thou canst not see him ?

JUNIPER. . . . Little Father ! . . . Little Father ! . . .

[*There follows a pause.*

VOICE. Has he answered ?

JUNIPER. Why should he answer ?   He 's here.

VOICE. Is that all thou canst say for thyself ? If not, speak on !

JUNIPER. I 've no more, Father.

VOICE. If any other hath charge or accusation to bring, let him speak now !

A MAN'S VOICE. Father, I was naked in sin ; this man clothed me.   I used him roughly ;   he thanked me.   I robbed him ; he was grateful to me.

VOICE. Any other ?

A WOMAN'S VOICE. Father, my husband was in prison for theft ;   we were starving.   This man, having nothing of his own, went to the altar, and, to his own hurt, took alms from God to satisfy our need.

VOICE. Any other ?

VOICE OF ELIAS. Father, this man feared me : I had authority ;   binding him to obedience I was cruel to him, despising his foolishness.   But when I myself became an outcast, then he forgave, then he prayed for me ;   and, serving me without fear, won for me pardon, penance, reconciliation.

VOICE. Is there any other ?

THE LAST COMMENT

VOICE OF FRANCIS. Father, when God in His mercy made man, He made few wise, but many foolish. Then sent He His Son, our Lord Jesus Christ, to be understood of fools better than of wise men. So, when He called me also to His service, the better to understand Christ and His Love for all, He gave me this fool for example and guide, for rest, and for refreshment. And because of him, in dark nights I found my way, and on long journeys failed not : so lived—he helping me !

VOICE. That is past, Brother. What use hast thou for him now, when all journeys are over, and nights ended ? Tell it, so that he may hear !

VOICE OF FRANCIS. O little sheep, hear my voice, make haste and come to me ! Yea, on holy obedience, I bid thee come !

JUNIPER. Name of Jesus ! . . . Little Father !

[*Very dimly the form of* JUNIPER *is seen to rise up from the bed, and advance to where, in the midst of the tribunal,* ST. FRANCIS *is waiting for him ; and all at once, in a burst of song, voice answering voice, an old memory grows young again.*

FRANCIS and JUNIPER.

City of Nineveh,
City of Nineveh,
Look upon Juniper !
Look upon Juniper !
Great is his foolishness,
Great is his foolishness,
Like unto charity,
Like unto charity.

[JUNIPER *has arrived.* FRANCIS *lays his arm over*

213

the shoulder of JUNIPER *and draws him in. Their voices become lost among the voices of others; but the song that is sung is still their song.*

OMNES. Nineveh, Nineveh,
What are you weeping for?
Blindness and hardness of heart without charity.
Nineveh, Nineveh,
What are you seeking for?
Juniper's foolishness, prize above rubies.
Prize above rubies;
Take and spend it!
Nothing can equal it;
Nothing can mend it.
Pearls before swine it is;
Find it or lose it!
Sweeter than wine it is;
Therefore I choose it!

[*The scene closes in again; once more one sees bare walls, a* Watcher *rousing from sleep, and on the bed the body of* JUNIPER *with arms wide. The* BROTHER SACRISTAN *enters, looks, crosses himself, kneels, and prays. The other* Brother, *waking, suddenly kneels also.*

CURTAIN

214

THE LAST DISCIPLE

(1270)

St. Francis has been dead many years; and BROTHER LEO, *the loved disciple, now old and feeble, is near his end. Persecuted by the Superiors of the Order for a too-faithful following of his master's teaching, he has become something of an outlaw; and any of the Brothers who come to see him do so by stealth. He lies on a sack bed in a half-ruined hut, whose walls, roof, and doorless entrance let in the day. It is late afternoon; the fields outside wear the fresh green of spring, and the hillside beyond glows bright under a sky darkening for rain.*

In the gloom of the hut, the stretched and motionless body lies almost unnoticeable; till, feebly and with pauses, his voice makes itself heard.

LEO. Little Father. . . . Little Father. . . .

[*Through a rift of cloud a ray of level sunlight strikes in, making the interior bright for a few moments before it passes. By intonation alone, with no raising of the voice, the* Old Man *begins singing.*

Praised be my Lord for all being;
And namely praise for our brother Sun,
Who bringeth us day, and light for seeing:
With joy he cometh his course to run.

[*After a pause, in the once more darkened interior, he begins speaking—words of St. Francis, which he remembers.*

Therefore, let no man say, ' I love God,' if he do not the will of God ; or if he give not his body unto pain of death, that so God's will be done in him—if, by infirmity, of himself he cannot. So in his weakness shall the power of Love be made known ; so shall the Kingdom of Heaven be also in men's hearts (which see darkly) as where, in light celestial, seraphs do behold Him face to face.

[*While he speaks there is a sound of approaching sheep-bells ; a young* SHEPHERD, *carrying a pitcher and a spray of hawthorn, halts outside the door, and stands, half fearful, listening. Only when the words pass into silence does he find courage to enter.*

SHEPHERD. I 've come again, Brother. Here 's water and bread ; and here 's that other thing you asked for. There 's plenty of it about now : hill-sides white with it.

[*He sets down the pitcher and loaf, and lays the blossoming branch on* LEO'S *bed. Very feebly* LEO'S *hand goes out to touch it. The* SHEPHERD *stands watching.*

[*After waiting awhile for the other to speak.*] Is that all you want, Brother ?

LEO. I thank you, Brother. That is all.

SHEPHERD. And you don't mind being out here all alone, when it gets dark ? I should be afraid.

LEO [*after a long pause*]. I am not alone, Brother.

[*The* SHEPHERD *looks round him, a little scared. He shifts to the door, anxious to get away.*

216

SHEPHERD. I 'll look in again, when I 've got the sheep in—if it hasn't gone dark. To-morrow I 'll come early.

LEO. Do, Brother. God give you peace; and your sheep also.

SHEPHERD. I 've not to complain. This season we 've done well. . . . It looks a bit like storm.

> [*He goes; at intervals his voice is heard in the field, calling the sheep.*

LEO [*holding up the spray, sings*].

> Praised be my Lord for Mother Earth;
> > Us she holdeth in care and keep;
> And divers herbs she bringeth to birth,
> > Flowers to array, and grass to reap.

> > [*Outside there is a faint roll of thunder; it begins to rain.*

> Praised be my Lord for Sister Water,
> > Ever of service hath she been:
> Waiting on men, sweet running water;
> > She is humble, and precious, and clean.

> > [*Feebly he raises himself, dips, drinks; then lies watching the rain.*

Ah! There, there it still comes; and there 's joy in it! . . . Run, sister, run! I shall never see you again.

> [*The sun shines out; the rain continues.*

Now there 's a rainbow somewhere—but I can't see it. . . . And yet, I do.

> [*Too weak to support himself any longer, he falls back, and lying in shadow sees the sunlight striking the wall above his head. And again he speaks words that he remembers spoken by St. Francis in his last hour.*

> O Brother Sun,
> Rejoicing thou dost run
> Unto all lands !
> Therefore I bid thee take
> This heart in thy hands,
> Of a poor little one
> Whose journeyings are all done !

[*Suddenly his voice becomes urgent, and pitiful.*

Father Francis ! . . . Little Father, little Father, pray for me ! . . .   [*After a pause he continues.*

> And when thou dost make
> To rise from thy wings
> A new East, and dost wake
> (For our dear Lord's sake),
> Where new day begins,
> Beast, reptile, and bird,
> Cattle, and herd,
> And all creeping things :
> Then cry for me,
> Unto all thou dost see,
> ' On a Tree of great mercy,
> Christ died for thee ! ' . . .

Little Father . . . little Father ! . . . O love of St. Francis, pray for me !

> [*Outside the hut appears* SISTER GIACOMINA *in cloak and hood. She stands for a moment to listen, then enters.* BROTHER LEO *starts, as though a vision had come in answer to his prayer. She throws back her hood, and is recognised. Older than* BROTHER LEO, *she has still the life and vigour which he lacks, and the expression of her withered face is radiant and serene.*

218

GIACOMINA. What, Brother, still all alone?

LEO. No, Sister.

> [*His hand feebly raises the spray.*

GIACOMINA. Well, well, well! Whose good thought was that?

LEO. The shepherd, who folds in that field, brought it. Every day he comes once, sometimes twice, and brings water and bread. And often in the field I hear him, or his sheep. . . . Then you come. . . . No, Sister, I am never alone.

GIACOMINA. Could I come more often, I would, little Brother.

LEO. Do not wish it, little Sister. Let all be— as it is.

GIACOMINA. Must I not wish but as *you* wish? Come, Brother, let me wish as I like. Here, under my hand, I have brought a new wish with me to-day; one waiting without, that has long wished, and now begs that he may speak with you.

LEO. With me? Why, Sister?

GIACOMINA. Three days since, he heard the call, and has become a tertiary. Are you well enough? Will you see him?

LEO. I will see any that wishes to see me.

> [GIACOMINA *goes to the door; and at her call a young* NOVICE *enters.*

GIACOMINA. Come in!

LEO. God give you peace, Brother!

> [*The* NOVICE *approaches; he kneels, and, kissing* LEO'S *hand, remains silent.*

LEO. You wish to see me. What is your need?

NOVICE. O Lover of St. Francis, speak to me!

GIACOMINA [*preparing to leave them*]. Shall I go?

NOVICE. No, Sister; for you also have seen and known. My heart is hungry, Brother. Of our Father, the blessed Francis, tell me all you know!

LEO. All that I know? My time now is too short—for that, Brother.

NOVICE. A little—something to make me understand! You—oh, you that knew him!

LEO. What shall we tell, Sister?

GIACOMINA. Tell him we both are old; and yet his heart in us stays young. . . . Was he not beautiful?

LEO. God, to blind eyes and sinners, gave grace to think so!

GIACOMINA. He was a conqueror!

LEO. Of hearts: servant to all.

GIACOMINA. Was rich!

LEO. Possessing nothing.

GIACOMINA. Was wise.

LEO. Yet had no learning.

GIACOMINA. His love was wonderful!

LEO. Passing the love of women.

GIACOMINA. He did God's will—looking for no reward.

LEO. His love was a light, that came we saw not whence; and from us passed—whither we knew, but saw not.

GIACOMINA. He had joy in all his afflictions.

LEO. Was patient to men's reproaches.

GIACOMINA. Won enemies by kindness.

LEO. Bore all men's burdens.

GIACOMINA. Shared each man's sorrow.

LEO. Rejoiced in all rejoicing.

GIACOMINA. Was glad to live.

LEO. Yet was more glad to die.

GIACOMINA. Recovered the lost.

LEO. Comforted the forsaken.

GIACOMINA. Healed lepers.

LEO. Loved sinners.

[*For a moment the two lovers cease speaking, their love has gone beyond words.*

NOVICE. And you both knew him!

GIACOMINA. He was my dearest friend.

LEO. He was my brother, and father.

NOVICE. Oh, tell me more! for everything, as you speak, sounds wonderful. . . . And he, too, once a sinner!

LEO. Aye: by God's mercy, he knew sin well; so knew how to help sinners!

[LEO *lies rapt in thought for which he has no word.* GIACOMINA *takes up the tale.*

GIACOMINA. He was of the Kingdom of Heaven, and like a little child. All who followed, who listened to him, became also like children. All loved him.

NOVICE. Oh! tell me more!

LEO. His was the joyful heart, Brother.

GIACOMINA. Often he sang. When he laughed, all who heard laughed with him.

LEO. He taught us the wisdom of foolishness. Many can understand the wise and prudent, Brother, when what they say is clear. But he understood fools: he was patient and loved them. 'A good fool,' he said, 'is a great work of mercy, and well-pleasing to God.'

GIACOMINA. 'Become a brother,' he said: 'then you will understand.'

LEO. He knew mysteries that none dared ask to share—saw what no other could see. One saw him lifted to Heaven : but when he came back to earth he was simple. One day a man came to lie to him —to deceive him ; but remained to speak the truth. He confessed himself. The little Father said, ' It is *my* fault, Brother, that you should ever have thought of deceiving me.' He asked forgiveness of the sinner who confessed. . . . To all sinners, however great, he said ' Pray for me ! '

[LEO *becomes speechless.* GIACOMINA *comes to the rescue, and takes up the tale.*

GIACOMINA. He was but a youth when first I saw him, partner in his father's trade. When next I came, I found him and two friends building together : Francis, Leo, Bernard. All the world now sees that building, which goes building still.

LEO. He laid the foundation of it : poverty, love, charity, obedience. That is all he did, Brother— that it might last. If others do otherwise, the work will fail.

NOVICE. Did he say, Brother, that we must possess—*nothing* ?

LEO. He did not say it only : it was his life. ' Possess not, and be free ; have nothing : give all.' From that came joy, peace, power. The world is weak, through having great possessions. Thence come fear, war, anger, strife, cruelty, jealousy, hatred, destruction, death. . . . Death !

NOVICE. How did he live, Brother—possessing nothing ?

LEO. Even as you see a star, stationed alone in Heaven. It has no feet, no hands to aid it : only the power of God motions, uplifts, and keeps it placed. So he . . .

THE LAST DISCIPLE

                    [GIACOMINA *gives him water.*
                    And as a star,
Found by the rising day, faints to the eye,—
Becomes invisible, yet lives on still—
There, though one sees it not, a flame of fire,
Angelic, in unseen ministry : so he.

GIACOMINA.
We cannot show him, Brother.   With our best will,
So little can be told.

LEO.
                    All that he did,
Or said, or suffered—sorrowed or found joy in :
It means no more than—as when the world was
        made,
God gave it form, and voice, and sound, and
        motion,
To do His will : and yet the world meant nothing—
Till, in it, Christ was born.   So, Christ in him,
Brother.   Of that he died, and is gone hence,
Raised to the light invisible, that mine eyes
Cannot contain !
                    [*His voice breaks with weakness.*
GIACOMINA. Rest, Brother, rest awhile !

LEO.
In the dark places of my soul, he was a star !
The star went from me : there he still remains
Where the Light received him !

NOVICE.
O Brother Leo, O Father, you who knew,
Loved, watched by, tended, touched him whom I seek
With such poor understanding, lay your hand
Upon my head and heart : before you go,
Give me your blessing !

LEO [*laying hands*].

His, Brother, his! Own nothing! That is riches.
Listen, nay, listen, Brother: here is something
That I have held—too long! Come, take it from
    me!

    [*He opens his vest and draws out a small folded
        packet suspended by a cord.*

    NOVICE [*taking it*].

What is it, Brother, Father?

    GIACOMINA [*her voice breaking*].

Oh, what a giving is this!
Now shines thy star.

    LEO.

Here, from my heart, this from his heart which
    came,
Take, take! O little Father! Possession goes:
And only love is left!

    [*Kissing the packet, he looses, and lays it in the
      YOUNG MAN'S hand.*

                [*His voice sinks to a whisper.*
                    In a dark hour
With this he wrought salvation, when in despair
And desolation of spirit I lay bound,
Outcast, a soul forsaken: because one man
I loved more than my Maker. So mortal a love
Burned in my breast; there it became a torch
In the hand of the Evil One. Hell opened her
    mouth.
God shut His Face from me. Through cover of
    night,
Searching he found me—with his own hand wrote
    this,
And gave it to me. Read!

NOVICE [*reading*]. ' The Lord bless and keep thee.
The Lord make His face to shine on thee. The
Lord lift up the light of His countenance upon
thee, and give thee peace. . . . Brother Leo, the
Lord bless thee, as thou hast blessed me.'

LEO.
So having written, he read : then said to me,
' When thou art in trouble, show this to Brother
    Sin.'

NOVICE. Brother Sin !

LEO.
' Do not be afraid,' he said, ' of Brother Sin.
He is a leper : but when thou hast washed his
    feet,
Then shalt thou see, in them, the wounds of Christ.
Yea, when for us Christ died—with Him
Died also Brother Sin.'
    [*The* NOVICE *presses the writing to his lips ;*
        then folds, and lays it away in his bosom.
Thus did he help me.   Take it, little Brother ;
'Tis all I have.   When thou 'rt in trouble, show
    this
To Brother Sin. . . . Go, and God give you peace !
    [*Without a word, the* NOVICE *kneels, takes his*
        blessing, kisses his hand, and goes.

GIACOMINA. He is gone, Brother.

LEO.
Has come : is one of us !   Our sure possession :
The Light which leads, he follows—and will find,
Though many miss the way, where my feet fail.
The Order has cast me out ; yet there remains
The Brotherhood, whose head and corner-stone,
Walls, roof, and door, are all set up in Christ. . . .

And these poor hands had once part in that building,
Whose top has reached to Heaven !   Now, as men
    build,
Confusion drowns their tongues.   But we—that heard
Pentecost come again, where each man's language,
Into each heart, by one man's lips was uttered—
We know the speech of Paradise is one,
And cannot be divided. . . .

           [In the distance a bell begins tolling.
             . . . See ! it grows dark.
You stay too late, Sister ; you must go home.

    GIACOMINA.

In a while, Brother : when we have said all
We have to say.   Hark !   There is a sweet sound :
There is a company, that, unconfounded,
Sounds forth into the world !

    LEO. Aye ? . . . What is it ?

    GIACOMINA.

Yonder a bell which tolls the hour ; and here,
In the fold, sheep making music as they feed—
So many we cannot count them ; but the shepherd—
He counts not, for he knows.

    LEO. What is that water I hear ?

    GIACOMINA.

It comes from the hills :
The little torrents falling after the rain.
To-morrow, ere noon, they will be dry again,
But earth will have drunk, and will be satisfied.

    LEO. I too, then, shall have drunk—and shall be
satisfied !

    GIACOMINA.

If it must be so, Brother, is there nothing
That I can do—before : while yet there is time ?

LEO.

Time is from God, Sister; but goes not to Him
With us, when *we* go. . . . Farewell, Brother
    Time !

        [*There is silence between them for a while.*

  GIACOMINA. Shall I bring a priest, Brother ?

LEO.

Aye, if you will ; and if he is willing, Sister.
Tell him 'tis Brother Leo. If he will not—
Commend me unto others that know me better.

  GIACOMINA.

For that, I needs must leave you. You must be
    alone for a while.

  LEO. Not alone, Sister.

  GIACOMINA. God's peace be with you ! I shall be
back soon.   [*She goes out quickly.*

  LEO.

Soon . . . soon. . . . What is ' soon ' ? Soon all
    will be dark,
Darker than night. O Star that I cannot see !

    [*And now, in the gradually increasing darkness,
      the quiet recumbent figure becomes almost indis-
      tinguishable. Only a glimmer of light falls
      upon the face, and the voice, with pauses now
      and again for weakness, or meditation, goes
      slowly on.*

Domine, Domine, Deus salutis meae, in die
clamavi, et nocte coram te. Redime me, Domine,
et miserere mei.

    [*Then again, with voice scarcely above a whisper,
      he sings.*

      Praised be my Lord for all who give
        Pardon to others for His Love's sake,

And meekly endure in pains to live :
    In Him they rest ; in Him shall wake.

[*He speaks.*

Miserere mei, Deus, secundum magnam misericordiam tuam ! Exaudi me : intende voci meae,
cum clamavero ad te !   [*He sings.*
    Praised be my Lord for Sister Death. . . .
    No mortal body shall she spare.
    Woe, if in sin man perisheth !
    For him the pains of Hell lie there.

[*He speaks.*

Pains of Hell ! . . . Death. . . . I am afraid. . . .
Little Father ! . . . Little Father ! . . . I cannot
find thee : hold me ! let me know ! . . . Take !
Take ! . . . Enough, no more. Live, Lucio, live !
. . . I *have* lived, Brother. . . . Kiss me, Francesco.
. . . I thank thee for my life ! . . . Thy pardon,
Brother : who art thou ? . . . Not my feet only,
but my hands and head. . . . My feet first, Brother.
. . . Eripe me, Domine, ab homine malo ; a viro
iniquo, eripe me ! Intret oratio mea in conspectu
tuo, Domine ; ostende mihi, Domine, misericordiam
tuam.

[*Then there is silence. Dark against the gloom
    of the outside twilight, the* SHEPHERD *comes,
    stands in the doorway and listens.*

SHEPHERD. Brother . . . Brother. . . . Is any
one there ? . . . Is any one there—alive ? . . . Oh !
    [*Scared by the silence, he turns and runs.*

LEO [*starting up*]. Little Father ! Little Father !
. . . Did I not hear thee call ? . . . Oh, star ! . . .
    [*But the star he sees now is not the one that he
        desires : he lies down again.*

228

O little Father, whom I so loved, body and soul—
now take me, body and soul, Shepherd of sheep !
and lead me where I know not ! . . . Lead me from
thought, from wish, from love of thee ; away from
fellow-man to Maker Christ. . . . In Him let me
find light ! . . . Dark, all is dark. . . . De profundis clamavi ad te, Domine, Domine, exaudi
vocem meam. Si iniquitates observaveris, Domine,
Domine, quis sustinebit ! . . . Bread, bread, Brother !
. . . Man is His making ! . . . O Jesu Christ,
make me ! . . . O Lord, Lover Christ, when saw
we Thee hungry, sick, poor, in prison ? . . . Go not
far from me, O Lord ! O Lord, hear my voice ! . . .
Take ! . . . Take ! . . . Take ! . . . The Lord make
His face to shine upon thee. Brother Leo, the Lord
bless thee as thou hast blest me ! . . . Show this
to Brother Sin. . . . O Maker Christ ! . . . crucified,
. . . dead . . . buried . . . descended . . . rose again
. . . communion of saints . . . forgiveness of sins. . . .
Through my fault, my own fault, my own most
grievous fault. . . . Forgive me, Brother Sin. . . .
No light . . . no light . . . no light. . . . And
yet I see !

> [*His voice ceases. It is so dark one does not
> see him die. Outside are footsteps ; the light
> of a lantern is seen approaching.* GIACOMINA
> *enters, followed by a* Priest, *and a* Friar
> *bearing the light.*

GIACOMINA. This way, Father. Brother, bring
in the light ! . . . There he lies, Father. . . . We
are come, Brother.

> [*She approaches the bed, and kneels
> beside it.*

Brother Leo! . . . Brother Leo!

[*The light of the lantern falls on the dead face.*

PRIEST [*making the sign of the Cross*]. Requiem aeternam dona ei, Domine ; et lux perpetua luceat ei. [*Over the dead body he raises the Host.*] Corpus Domini nostri, Jesu Christi, custodiat animam tuam in vitam aeternam.

CURTAIN

NOTE

Certain passages in this play have reference to earlier plays, in which Brother Leo, previous to his religious calling, has appeared under the name of Lucio Leone.